From the publishers of California Diving News

Southern California's
Best Beach Dives

By Dale and Kim Sheckler

D1245211

Special Thanks to:
Mary Lou Reed
Michael Letteriello

The divers of California,
and Southern California Dive Stores

All photographs by Dale and/or Kim Sheckler

Copyright © 1991 by Saint Brendan Corporation, all rights reserved

Saint Brendan Corporation
P.O. Box 11231, Torrance, CA 90510
(310) 792-2333

Printing by Quality Lithograph, Torrance, CA

Special Note: the descriptions in this book are not scientific facts. The diver's final decisions and actions are their responsibility. The publishers and authors of this book assume no responsibility of any mishap claimed to be a result of this book.

First Edition: 1986
Second Edition: 1991
Second Printing 1993
Third Printing 1994

ISBN 0-9628600-0-X

Dedication:
To our boys,
Christopher, Reed, and Eric -
May they always delight in the sea

CONTENTS

Dive Spots At A Glance

	COUNTY	VISIBILITY	GAME	FACILITIES	ACCESS	ENTRY	SNORKELING
TAJIGUAS	SB	G	F	N	E	E	G
REFUGIO	SB	G	F	T/S	E	E	G
ARROYO BURRO	SB	F	P	T	E	E	F
MESA LANE	SB	VG	G	N	D	E	G
SANTA CRUZ ST.	SB	G	F	N	D	M	G
BILTMORE STEPS	SB	F	F	N	E	E	G
DEER CREEK RD.	VEN	F	G	N	E	E	F
LEO CARRILLO	LA	G	G	T/S	E	E	G
EL MATADOR	LA	G	VG	T	D	E	F
CORRAL BEACH	LA	F	F	T	E	E	F
BIG ROCK	LA	F	F	N	E	M	F
LAS TUNAS	LA	F	F	N	E	E	F
REDONDO CANYON	LA	G	P	T/S	E	E	P
OLD REDONDO PIER	LA	G	P	T/S	M	E	F
RAT BEACH	LA	P	F	N	M	M	F
MALAGA COVE	LA	F	G	N	E	M	G
HAGGERTY'S	LA	G	G	N	VD	D	G
FLAT ROCK	LA	G	VG	N	VD	D	G
CHRISTMAS TREE	LA	VG	G	N	VD	D	G
POINT VICENTE	LA	F	F	T	D	D	G
OLD MARINELAND	LA	G	F	N	E	M	G
WHITE POINT	LA	F	P	T	E	E	G
NEWPORT PIER	OR	F	P	T/S	E	E	F
CORONA BREAKWATER	OR	F	F	T/S	E	E	G
LITTLE CORONA	OR	G	G	T/S	M	E	G
REEF POINT	OR	G	G	T/S	E	E	G
SHAW'S COVE	OR	G	P	N	E	E	G
FISHERMAN'S COVE	OR	G	G	N	E	E	G
DIVER'S COVE	OR	G	R	N	E	E	G
PICNIC BEACH	OR	G	R	T/S	E	E	G
ROCKY BEACH	OR	G	R	T	E	E	G
MAIN BEACH	OR	F	R	T/S	E	E	G
CRESS STREET	OR	F	G	N	E	M	G
WOODS COVE	OR	G	G	N	E	E	G
MOSS STREET	OR	G	G	N	E	E	G
1,000 STEPS	OR	F	G	T/S	D	M	G
LA JOLLA CANYON	SD	G	R	T/S	E	E	P
GOLDFISH POINT	SD	G	R	N	D	E	G
LA JOLLA COVE	SD	G	R	T/S	E	E	G
CHILDREN'S POOL	SD	G	F	T/S	E	E	G
HOSPITAL POINT	SD	F	F	N	E	M	F
N. MISSION BEACH JETTY	SD	F	G	T/S	E	D	F

SB: Santa Barbara
VEN: Ventura
LA: Los Angeles
OR: Orange
SD: San Diego

P: Poor
F: Fair
G: Good
VG: Very Good
R: Ecological Reserve,
   no game to be taken

E: Easy
M: Moderate
D: Difficult
VD: Very Difficult

N: None
T: Toilets
S: Showers

Introduction

Beach diving in Southern California can be rewarding, exciting and just plain fun. You simply need to know where to go. Much of the coastline along Southern California is neither fit nor fun to dive. Then again, many locations offer excellent diving in clear, life-filled waters and are very easy to reach. To repeat: You simply need to know where to go. That is the purpose of this book. It is meant to be a highly-detailed dive guide of the best beach diving along the Southern California coastline.

The criteria for a beach location to be considered a "best beach dive" are simple: First, the dive spot must have consistently good visiblity. If it averages 10 to 15 feet or better year round, it is a good standard. Many locations along the coast will reach and exceed that standard from time to time but if the water clarity is unpredictable, the dive spot does not qualify. If you are like most sport divers in California, water visibilty need not be spectacular to have a good time but you probably need a minimum of 10 feet to make the dive an enjoyable one.

Secondly, there must be a wide variety of things to see and do at the dive spot. Fifty-foot visiblity is great but if there is nothing to see but sand, the dive can get boring quickly. While not all dive spots described in this book are open to hunting (some fall into marine or ecological preserves), the underwater photographer, explorer, or general sightseer will enjoy most of them.

All of the dive spots that have been reviewed are within 100 to 150 yards off shore; many are very close to the water's edge. Long swims are not necessary to find excellent diving along the Southern California coastline; however, most of these dive spots do have good diving farther out for those who choose to dive the more remote reefs and locations.

Easy access to the shore is another important consideration, but a few exceptions have been made. Several of the locations along Palos Verdes, for example, have poor access but the diving off these spots is so good that their attention is warranted. At some of the locations, driving your car almost to water's edge is possible, where others require some climbing on steep but safe trails and stairs. Ultimately, only you can best judge your climbing ability.

Some final considerations in qualifying a shore location as a "best beach dive" can include crowds (or lack thereof), facilities, game, currents, average surf conditions, and how well the location is known. Several locations such as 1,000 Steps in Orange County and El Matador Beach in Los Angeles County are only known to the local divers yet these spots offer superb diving that is well worth the drive from outside the area.

Almost all of these dive spots are worth the drive of a few hours. Many of the locations are very unusual. The vertical drops of La Jolla Canyon and the tall, life-covered pilings at Old Redondo Pier #3 are good examples of underwater terrain that is hard to find elsewhere along the coast.

Almost all known dive spots—good or bad—are listed in the introduction sections of each county. If you are a more advanced diver, many of the locations not described may be rewarding to you. With over three dozen dive spots detailed in this book, you could dive a different location every other weekend for nearly two years. You can explore several of the dive sites over and over again and never cover the same area twice.

There are some important things to remember about this book. As good as many of this spots are, all are subject to local ocean and weather conditions. The dive spots listed in this book will, more often than not, have good diving, but all spots along the coast have their bad days. Water will be dirty after rain in most spots and high surf will pound good dive spots along with the bad. To avoid wasted trips, always call the surf report before leaving home and have an alternate dive site in mind.

The final decision to make the dive or not is yours. KNOW YOUR LIMITATIONS! Many of the dive spots in this book are very easy to dive, but all require some degree of skill. Only you can judge your ability to deal with surf and local conditions.

Finally, this book is as accurate as possible. Underwater features are close approximates at best. Storms and time change the face of the coastline and ocean bottom constantly. Facilties can also change through additions or renovations. This is the most detailed dive guide of this type ever attempted, but keep the changes of time in mind.

Armed with this book you will have years of excellent beach diving ahead of you. Dive safe and enjoy!

Beach Diving Tips

Beach diving in Southern California can and should be an enjoyable experience with some of the world's finest diving lying off this coastline. Of course, beach diving cannot beat the ease, convenience and quality of boat diving; however, beach diving does have some advantages over boat diving. It's cheap and you can dive when you want to and as long as you wish. To make beach diving just as enjoyable as boat diving, a few simple steps in preparation and diving techniques are needed, none of which requires a great deal of time or expense.

The first step in preparation should be awareness of your physical conditioning. It doesn't take a great deal of physical prowess to beach dive in Southern California but you should be able to run around the block a couple of times without problem. Most of the dive sites in this book are easy with short swims of 150 yards or less. The best way to get into shape for beach diving is some kind of aerobic exercise: running, cycling, dance, or preferably swimming. Try to do a lot of just plain hard kicking with fins. Emphasizing again, it does not take a lot of physical strength to make a beach dive in calm conditions, but

you must have enough stamina to get you in and out of the water, get you to your offshore destination, and adequately handle any emergency that may arise. You are the final judge of your capabilities.

The next step of preparation takes place before ever leaving home. Check your gear thoroughly. Make sure mask and fin straps are in good condition and fit snugly. Weight belt buckles should secure the weight belt tightly as well. These are good points to check for any type of diving. Extra pieces of gear to consider carrying on a beach dive include a flag and float (required in some areas and always a good idea) and a blanket, tarp or sheet to lay across the sand to place your gear.

Always call the surf and/or dive report before leaving home. This will give you a general idea as to what to expect on arriving at the beach. If the surf is up at one beach, it may be almost nothing at another. A fine example is when the southerly swells are hitting Laguna Beach and Malibu hard, the west facing (Torrance and Redondo Beach) beaches in Santa Monica Bay are often well protected and fairly calm. Some of the "surf/dive" report phone numbers are very complete, offering reports on visibility and surge conditions.

Keep your ears glued to weather reports for "Santa Ana" wind conditions. Santa Ana Winds blow from the northeast or, in other words, from the land out to sea. These winds blow dirty nearshore waters out to sea to be replaced with cool, clean waters from the depths in an effect known as upwelling. The winds also tend to lay the surf down. The results of several days of Santa Ana Winds is usually flat, calm, clear waters—in short, excellent diving conditions with water visibility that can exceed 50 feet. Santa Ana Winds are the most common in late fall through winter.

Try to plan your dives in the mornings. The seas tend to be calmer this time of day and the crowds thinner. Also try to plan dives during periods of high or incoming tides. The incoming tides bring in the clear offshore water creating better visibility. The higher water may also help in getting by any shallow reef on your swim out to the dive site. The rule of diving with the high tide does have its exceptions. Some beaches are impassable during high tide and the surf may be more difficult to deal with. Use these rules as a guideline but don't revolve your dive plans around them.

Upon arrival at the beach, take the time to observe conditions carefully. Many dive sites offer high vantage points in which observation of the ocean conditions below are excellent. Before ever putting on any gear, scout the dive site carefully. Bring a pair of binoculars, if available; they may reveal hidden reefs or kelp. Watch the surf carefully. Surf will often come in "sets" of two to five big waves followed by periods of two to ten minutes of small waves. Time these sets.

Look for rip currents. A rip current is a free ticket offshore if you use it properly. Carefully check entry and exit points and always have an alternate. Consider making a rock entry as opposed to a sand beach entry; it may save a lot of swimming. Look at the way the kelp is laying; this is a good indication of currents. And last but not least, be sure to check out what members of the opposite sex you will impress on the beach with your diving. Check carefully with the binoculars.

Kidding aside, you will, most likely, decide at this point if the particular dive spot and present conditions are for you. KNOW YOUR LIMITATIONS! You must ask yourself, "Will I enjoy a dive here today?" If not, seek an alternate dive spot or activity. Struggling in conditions that are past your comfort level will not be fun, and at worst, may also be dangerous.

Unless you have a long walk to the beach and plan to rest before entering the water, dress completely at the car, mask and fins excluded. If you don't, you will merely have to dress again on the beach, wasting time and energy. Use caution in your descent to the beach. Even safe-looking stairs can be hazardous with a lot of extra gear on.

On the beach, carefully discuss again the dive plan with your buddy. Agree on entry and exit points, alternate exit point, etc. Check each other's gear thoroughly. Get all gear completely in place. To go into the surf without fins on and your mask on your face means almost certain loss of gear. Always have all gear in place before entering the water.

Time the wave "sets" again; also time the wave "interval." Waves will come in intervals of 5 to 20 seconds. You will want to enter the water between the "sets" and during the wave "interval." Properly done, it is not unusual to be able to get past a short surf zone without ever being touched by a wave.

When entering the surf zone, waste no time. Do not stop to adjust gear or look back. Swim out just past the surf then rest. You will reduce your odds of getting knocked down considerably. Should you get knocked down, stay down. If the water is deep enough to swim (two to three feet deep) kick out the rest of the way. Many experienced divers wade out to water this deep and turn to swim. Take the larger waves by going underneath them. If you time your entry properly and don't stop in the surf zone, odds are you will have none of these problems.

Exiting the water is a reverse of the above. Approach the seaward side of the surf zone as close as possible and wait there. Relax and catch your breath. To repeat, time the waves. Between wave sets and in the interval is the time to go for shore. Waste no time and don't stop. Again, if done properly, you may reach shore and never be touched by a wave. When you reach waist-deep water, stand up and back out the remainder of the way keeping your eye on the surf. If you get knocked down or can't get up, stay down and crawl in.

Consider making a rock entry, it can sometimes save a lot of swimming. With the proper conditions, a rock entry is nearly as simple as rolling off a boat. This kind of entry does require some training; however, and an advanced class is highly recommended. Another recommended course is the 3R's classes (Rocks, Reefs, and Rips).

With a little experience, guidance, and by diving the best spots (that's what this book is all about), you will find yourself becoming an avid and regular beach diver. Why? Because beach diving is fun and enjoyable.

Introduction to Santa Barbara / Ventura Counties

To most regional divers, the foremost attraction in the Santa Barbara/Ventura area is its beautiful offshore islands. For this reason, the large majority of this area's shore-diving spots are somewhat ignored. These locations offer easy accessibility, superb diving conditions, plentiful game, and beautiful underwater scenery. If you have only a few hours to spare or you don't want to spend the money on a boat trip, these dive spots are worth looking into. If you aren't from the Santa Barbara/Ventura County area, you might consider exploring these spots. They are well worth the trip.

Diving the Santa Barbara County coastline can be quite different from coastal diving farther south. Perhaps the largest noticeable difference is in the types and varieties of sea life. Colors and sizes are more varied and every crevice and rock seems to hold a surprise.

From the San Luis Obisbo/Santa Barbara County line southward, around Point Arguello and Point Conception, there is little or no coastal access with the exception of Jalama Beach County Park, north of Point Conception. Point Conception has been called the "Cape Horn of

Santa Barbara/San Luis Obisbo County Line

Santa Barbara County Surf Report: (805) 962-SURF
Ventura County Surf Report: (805) 644-8338

Map not to scale • Not for navigation

N

Pt. Arguello

Jalama

Hwy. 101

Pt. Conception

Gaviota

Tajiguas

Refugio

El Capitan

Isla Vista

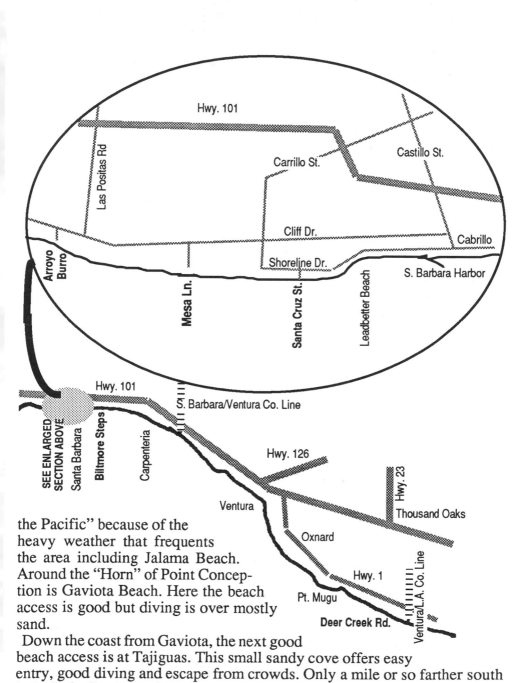

the Pacific" because of the heavy weather that frequents the area including Jalama Beach. Around the "Horn" of Point Conception is Gaviota Beach. Here the beach access is good but diving is over mostly sand.

Down the coast from Gaviota, the next good beach access is at Tajiguas. This small sandy cove offers easy entry, good diving and escape from crowds. Only a mile or so farther south is Refugio State Beach with excellent facilities and good diving.

Continuing southward the diving runs into dirtier water. El Capitan State Beach, like Refugio, has excellent facilities but only average diving. The next nearest shore access is in the Isla Vista / Goleta Bay area but water visibility is only fair and the water is sometimes covered with oil from a natural seepage from nearby Coal Oil Point.

Arroyo Burro State Beach has cleaner water and good access. Although facilities at Arroyo are very good, they are lacking at Mesa Lane and Santa Cruz Street. Although the diving is some of the best Santa Barbara County has to offer, you'll have to work for it as each of these points have many stairs. Farther toward the harbor, there are other access points but water becomes progressively less clean. Leadbetter Beach, adjacent to the harbor breakwater, has some interesting reefs and good facilities but normally dirty water.

South of Santa Barbara Harbor, diving spots become more scarce. Patches of kelp mark small reefs along the coast. Some of these reefs can be found off Montecito where access is limited. Access is easy off the Santa Barbara Biltmore Hotel and a kelp forest lies near shore but visibility is only fair at best. Carpenteria Beach holds a larger reef but the best diving is a long swim away. At the Ventura County line is Rincon Beach Park for diving in generally poor visibility.

Most of the diving from Rincon southward to the city of Ventura is in poor visibility; but, possible dive spots in this area include Punta Gorda, offering diving with easy access on the pier that extends to the offshore artificial oil island. More oil piers to the south and offshore kelp present more diving opportunities.

Pierpoint Bay off the City of Ventura has little diving. The bottom is a gently sloping sand bottom and heavy surf is common. The sand beaches here and south of the harbor mouth offer diving for halibut and pismo clams only.

Proceeding southward after the mouth of Channel Islands Harbor is the mouth of Port Hueneme. Here lies the ill-fated luxury ship *La Jennelle*. The wreck was filled in with rock and, lying at the edge of Hueneme Submarine Canyon. This used to be one of the best beach dives in Southern California but the Navy has since rebuilt the fence bordering the dive site making access and water entry difficult.

South of Port Hueneme, access is limited and diving is mainly over sand until reaching Point Mugu. From Point Mugu, there are spotty offshore reefs, many of which are long swims. The one exception is at Deer Creek Road. Access here is easy and the kelp comes within 30 yards of shore.

Just before the Los Angeles County line and the Malibu area is another close-in reef near the intersection of Yerba Buena Road. However, this reef is more exposed to surf than the Deer Creek Road location and subject to heavy surge and thus many surfers.

A short distance down the road is Harrison's (County Line) Reef. Lying 300 yards offshore from the blue-roofed apartment buildings, a dive here is only for the good swimmer.

Tajiguas

Diving and other leisure activities abound at the state beaches along the coast north of Santa Barbara. It's easy to understand why. The state beaches offer excellent facilities including restrooms, camping, showers, and food services. Unfortunately, large crowds often come with the the comforts. If you want to escape the crowds and enjoy fine diving north of Santa Barbara, try Tajiguas.

Diving from the small sandy cove can be very rewarding. Rocky ledges lie directly off the beach and extend around the point to the west. The ledges begin in shallow water and extend into water over 40-feet deep running parallel to shore. Most of the rocks are low-lying, rising from the bottom three to five feet. What makes them interesting are the sometimes large overhangs they create. Some of these slabs of rock stick out as much as five feet creating homes for many colorful types of marine life in the underside and tops of these ledges.

Invertebrates are the most common. Corynactius anemones are in several clumps with hues ranging from yellow to pink to lavender. Other types of anemones include the white-spotted rose anemone with its striking red body and tentacles or the large rose anemone with white tentacles and deep red body. All of these make for excellent macro-photo material. Red and brown and California golden gorgonia are also present on the deeper reefs, but not

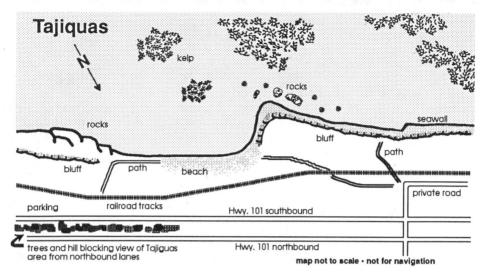

Tajiquas

N

kelp

rocks

rocks

seawall

bluff

bluff

path

path

beach

private road

parking   railroad tracks   Hwy. 101 southbound

trees and hill blocking view of Tajiguas
area from northbound lanes

Hwy. 101 northbound

map not to scale · not for navigation

in large numbers. The brilliant orange and blue Spanish shawl, and white and gold-horned nudibranchs make for interesting observation.

Fish are a little sparse in the area, but various rockfish find cover under the ledges, and some game fish find cover in the healthy kelp canopy.

Hunters will find little here. There are occasionally abalone and lobster present, but the area is usually well worked over. Scallops can be found on the

deeper and less-accessible reefs.

Access to the beach is easy off the southbound side of Highway 101. Parking and access is not visible from the northbound lanes. If traveling on the northbound lanes, turn around two miles north of Refugio State Beach. There is parking alongside of the highway on a dirt area. Access to the beach is via a dirt trail across the railroad tracks. The dirt path is gentle and safe. There are no facilities on the beach or near the parking area.

The best diving and entry is on the west end (far end) of the beach. Surfers congregate at the east end. Although most of the beach is sand, there are cobblestones in the surf, particularly in the winter.

Water conditions for Tajiguas are usually good. Visibility averages 10 feet and is often cleaner than beaches to the south due to a common mild current.

There is also access farther west on the road that leads to the west side of the point. Access here is steeper and more treacherous but the swim to some of the outer kelp is shortened.

Refugio State Beach

Refugio Beach beckons the leisure seeker. Under swaying palm trees, this secluded beach offers peaceful picnic facilities, excellent camping areas and good diving.

Refugio Beach is a state park complete with facilities such as 109 campsites, restrooms, showers and food. One could come here and have a thoroughly enjoyable time without even touching the water. But the water is why local divers make this a favorite spot.

Reefs and kelp lie off the beach only 50 yards out. The reefs offer a variety of terrain and sea life that will delight almost every diver. On the southeast end of the beach, near the camping area, kelp beds grow on a rock bottom from 10 to 20 feet deep. In calm weather, this area can be excellent for snorkeling. Beyond

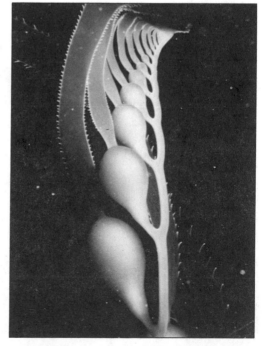

the kelp is a series of jagged rock ledges running parallel to shore. These ledges rise 12 feet from the bottom in spots and create interesting overhangs.

On these reefs are a wide variety of invertebrates, some of which may not be readily recognized by the the diver from the southern coastal waters. Nudibranchs are present in large numbers. Sea pansies dot the sand bottom and the odd sea porcupine or sea mouse can be found crawling about. Sea hares (sea slugs) are everywhere. Colorful anemones splash the reefs with color. In short, the rock ledges are a good area for the macro-photographer and sightseer.

In the kelp, only a few fish can be found. This is not a good area for game. Kelp bass in this area are very skittish and difficult to approach. No abalone are present on the near reefs on the eastern side of the beach. For game, one would have better luck to the northwest, up the coast and around the small point.

In this area, kelp is attached to low-lying reefs heavily silted in with sand. The depths of these reefs are between 15 and 25 feet. In the sections that are large enough to support them, an occasional abalone or lobster can be found; however, most are small. The long swim from the beach or hike to the point definitely requires a diver in good physical condition.

These and other nearby reefs can be reached by inflatable boat or kayak which can be easily launched from the beach in calm weather. Most of the parking is only a few gently-sloping yards from the beach.

Although the beach is somewhat protected from the northwest, it is a good

idea to call ahead to check conditions.

Refugio State Beach is approximately 25 miles north of Santa Barbara just off Highway 101. Exit 101 on the ramp indicating Refugio Beach. There is a day-use and camping fee. Call 1-800-444-7275 for camping reservations. Always follow the laws regarding the use of state parks. Proceed through the gate and, after passing under the railroad tracks, turn right for the northwest end of the beach and right for the southeast. There is ample parking close to water's edge.

In the summer, the burger stand is open for a between-dive snack.

The only disadvantage of this spot is summer crowds. If camping is in your plans, get reservations early. There is adequate parking year round for those using the beach for the day only.

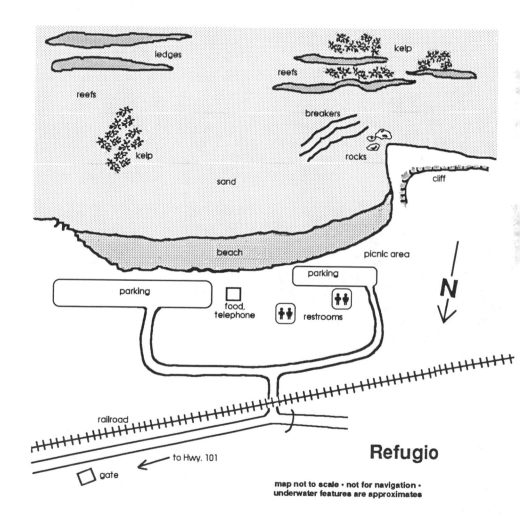

map not to scale · not for navigation ·
underwater features are approximates

Arroyo Burro State Beach

Probably the best diving, with the easiest access around the city of Santa Barbara, is off Arroyo Burro State Beach. This state beach lies neatly tucked into a small canyon about four miles north of the Santa Barbara Harbor. The beach is quite pleasant with picnic tables, restrooms, and even a small restaurant and snack bar. These amenities, along with plenty of parking, can at times attract heavy crowds. The beach is also used often by local instructors for check-out dives.

The best diving lies to the south off South Point. Diving off this point will require some walking but the beach is mainly sand, making the walk a pleasant one. Directly off the beach is mostly sand bottom. Offshore from South

Point are rocky ledges beginning as close as 25 to 50 yards out in 10 to 15 feet of water.

In deeper water, the ledges can become very colorful with anemones, nudibranchs and other invertebrates. Fish life include occasional garibaldi, lingcod, sheepshead, calico bass, and halibut. Other game is scarce.

Divers frequently use this area as a jumping-off point to reach Mohawk Reef, a large reef structure beginning at South Point and extending south past the Mesa Lane beach area. The best sections of this reef are, however, a long swim away. Because of Mohawk Reef, water clarity is usually best to the south with visibility averaging 15 feet.

There is no use fee or parking fee here and the park closes at 9:00 p.m.

Mesa Lane

To find beach diving with the best visibility off the city of Santa Barbara you will have to expend some energy. Because of an excellent reef structure, the diving off Mesa Lane is some of the best in the county, but, until just recently,

access to the diving here was limited to boats or mountain-goat divers who risked the steep, treacherous path that was once the only way to get to the beach. That path was replaced recently by a large number of safe, but long, steep stairs.

From the top of the stairs, an excellent view is offered of the diving area below. The beach is sand and rocks with a number of different entry and exit points. Offshore are kelp beds marking the best reefs. The large Mohawk Reef extends, in sections, from the north to the south.

Small reef begins within 25 to 50 yards of shore and extends in both directions along the coast. Kelp is 50 to 100 yards farther out.

All of the reefs in the area offer excellent underwater exploration. Small caves, huge rocks, large ledges and overhangs are common. Depths on the reefs vary from 10 to 15 feet on top to 25 to 30 feet on the bottom. Just outside the kelp, depths reach 40 feet. On the rocks and under the kelp is a large variety of sea life to delight the photographer and sightseer. The usually excellent water clarity also helps with photography and exploring. Visibility averages 15 to 20 feet and can reach 35 feet under the right conditions.

Hunters will enjoy this location as well. Gamefish such as lingcod, large sheepshead, and calico bass are common. Scallops and lobster also can be found although abalone is scarce.

Access begins at the end of Mesa Lane. There are no facilities.

Santa Cruz Street
(a.k.a. 1,000 Steps)

Tall, lush strands of kelp are broken up with patches and stretches of ivory sand. The rocky ledges are dotted with sprigs of color. Plenty of blue and purple color is provided by the urchins, so thick in spots, that from a distance, their spines give the illusion of a shag carpet stretching out across the reef.

Here and there, splotches of nature's bright blanket seem to be placed ever so carefully in order to provide delightful dashes of color. Donating the color are a variety of starfish, nudibranchs, and an occasional patch of anemones. Movement is provided by rockfish and thin senorita fish passing through the sunbeams like birds in a forest.

The walls of this magnificent room are the kelp. In places, solitary strands of kelp, regularly spaced from each other, appear as columns reaching for and supporting the amber translucent ceiling above. In reality the ceiling is floating and supporting the walls and columns. It is here, on clear, calm days, that the kelp forest in the shallow waters off Santa Cruz Boulevard in Santa Barbara provides one of the most beautiful coastal spots in Southern California.

Access to the beach is via 140 steps at the end of Santa Cruz Boulevard. Unfortunately, 140 steps can take on an ominous appearance to divers with 40 pounds of gear on their backs; consequently, the dive site has earned the nickname "1,000 steps." It's not as bad as it sounds, however, and very much worth it.

Limited parking can be found at the end of Santa Cruz Boulevard. There are no facilities here and private property abuts the stairway. Please be quiet and considerate of the residents. Public restrooms are available at Shoreline Park a block or so east on Shoreline Drive.

There is an excellent vantage point overlooking the kelp on the bluff. From there, ocean conditions can be assessed and a dive plan considered.

While overlooking the dive site, note the shallow reefs near the surf zone. Because of these rocks, this dive site is best during a high tide. Be aware, however, the beach here is very narrow and disappears entirely during an extreme high tide.

The shallow rocks are covered with thick eel grass that reaches to the surface. Swim through open channels on your way out to kelp to avoid entanglement.

From the beach, the bottom drops away at a gentle pace. Because this is a gently sloping bottom and a relatively shallow dive (10 - 25 feet deep), surf conditions can heavily affect the bottom. Surge is common. Call the local surf report phone number before heading for the beach. If the surf is three feet or larger, you'd be better off seeking out another deeper, more protected dive site.

But during calm days of little surf, particularly during the Santa Ana wind conditions, diving here can be superb. The Santa Anas are the winds that blow from the shore out to sea. They push the dirty surface water close to shore outward. Cool, clear deep waters move in to replace it. The result is low surf and visibility that can exceed 50 feet. The Santa Ana winds are most common during late fall and winter. During the these conditions visibility at Santa Cruz Boulevard runs between 30 and 50 feet. During other times of small or calm surf, visibility averages about 15 to 20 feet.

Regardless of the water clarity, you will find a lot to explore in this kelp forest. The bottom is varied with plenty of rocks, boulders and sand. An occasional rocky spire rises from the bottom providing interesting overhangs and mini-walls covered with life. Sand channels break up the kelp allowing sunlight to stream in here and there.

Hunting at this site is only fair. Spearfishermen will do well stalking rockfish on the reef and calico bass up among the kelp fronds. Halibut are less abundant but still available. Gathering on the bottom is less productive. Although rock scallops, lobster and abalone can be found, they are not abundant.

This is more of a site for sightseers and photographers. Photographers are often reluctant to carry their cameras on beach dives but, with proper precautions, a camera can be safely taken on beach dives. This dive site is good for both wide angle and macro shots. The kelp and fish provide good backdrops and subject material for wide angle work while patches of corynactis anemones, octopus, nudibranchs, and other invertebrates make for excellent closeup photo material.

Biltmore Steps

Built in 1927, the Biltmore Hotel has long been an elegant landmark on the Santa Barbara landscape. Overlooking the Santa Barbara Channel and the Northern Channel Islands beyond, the Santa Barbara Biltmore Hotel is one of the premier hotels of Southern California due mainly to its excellent location.

Directly in front of the hotel, just on the other side of Channel Drive, is a thin sand beach where hotel guests and honeymooners frequently stroll. But what many of them don't notice is the kelp bed lying offshore to the east.

The dive site at the Biltmore Hotel has easy access and good diving but is not well known outside the local Santa Barbara diving community. While this is certainly not the most exciting dive site along the Santa Barbara coastline, its removal from the crowds of the main beaches makes it an attractive alternative to other more popular and crowded dive sites.

The best diving lies at the extreme east end of the beach out from the historic Coral Casino (also owned by the hotel). There are two main reefs: an inner reef very close to shore and an outer kelp bed 100 to 200 yards out.

The sand beach here drops off quickly in depth to 15 feet. Because of this, the surf zone is narrow and the breakers are powerful plungers. This type of wave is good in that the surf zone is short and, with proper timing, it's easy to get out with little trouble. The bad news about plunging waves is they carry

much more of a wallop —picking divers up and dropping them suddenly to the beach. Time your water entries and exit carefully to coincide with wave sets and intervals.

The inner reef begins just beyond the surf line. The bottom is strewn with various-sized boulders covered with a mixture of eel grass and feather boa kelp. Eel grass and feather boa kelp does not break as easily as giant kelp so use caution in passage. There is some giant kelp on this inner reef but its presence and abundance is dictated by water conditions and recent storms.

Among these marine plants are large schools of surf perch and opaleye. For the spearfishermen, both calico and sand bass are abundant and large. Halibut can sometimes be found in the the sand adjacent to the reef. Other fish filling the waters around this inner reef include senoritas, kelpfish, and gobies.

Frankly, the rocks on this inner reef are not terribly exciting. For observing reef life, the outer kelp bed is much more interesting.

The outer kelp is a bit of a swim but worth it. Use caution on the swim out as boat traffic can occasionally be heavy. A suggested dive plan is to first descend on the inner reef after taking a compass heading for the outer kelp. Swim over to the outer kelp underwater. The sand flats between the two reefs are by no means dull. Marine life to be observed include thornback rays, halibut, sea pens, and sand stars. An occasional random boulder dots the sand flat.

The outer reef depths fall in the 20 to 25 foot range. Giant kelp is abundant and thick. Lucky divers may spot abalone or lobster among the crevices. Color is provided by small stands of golden gorgonia and bat stars. As with the inner reef, schools of perch, and some rather large opaleye, cruise the kelp trees.

Water conditions at this site are consistent but usually only fair. Visibility averages 10 to 15 feet. As the dive is relatively shallow, surf of three feet or over can stir up the bottom with surge. Plankton blooms can also affect visibility adversely. With the exception of the surge, currents are rare.

The easiest way to reach the Biltmore is to exit the 101 Freeway at Cabrillo Boulevard. Cabrillo intersects with Channel Drive almost immediately. Take Channel Drive east as it curves toward the beach. The beach is long and narrow with the most interesting diving at the east end adjacent to the Coral Casino. Parking is limited along the street and free. A few steps lead to the beach.

Deer Creek Road

On the extreme southern coastline of Ventura County, near Point Mugu, the shore becomes rugged and rocky with some small coves and stretches of sand beaches. Highway 1 comes very close to the water's edge in places but access is still limited. Where Deer Creek Road intersects with the highway, kelp beds

reach close to shore and there is easy stairway access to a sandy beach.

The thick kelp beds here are attached to a rocky reef with crevices, small caves and some large boulders. The kelp starts in 20 feet of water close to shore and extends out to depths of 30-35 feet over 200 yards out. The kelp and rocks support a large variety of life. On the rocks are nudibranchs, sponges, urchins, starfish, and occasionally some lobster and abalone. Rock scallops dot the rocks as well. In the kelp are calico bass, sheepshead, opaleye and other varieties of fish. Large halibut and rays can often be found lying in the sand adjacent to the reefs. Lucky divers may also encounter dolphins, seals or even migrating gray whales on the seaward side of the reef.

Although the reefs come in fairly close to shore, the better diving can be a moderate swim away. The spot is open to heavy surf and consequently surge and visibility on the bottom can be variable. With a two-three foot swell, visibility inside the kelp runs about 10 feet. Outside the reef, visibility runs 20-30 feet. A higher surf creates a bottom surge reducing visibility accordingly.

Beach access is easy via a short stairway off Pacific Coast Highway, immediately north of the intersection with Deer Creek Road. From the top of the stairs, you can see the series of kelp beds that lie 30 to 300 yards offshore. The stairs lead to a sandy beach where a surf entry is possible. Rock reefs without kelp are as close as 50 feet in 15 feet of water.

Although this area is close to Pacific Coast Highway, it is not frequented by others due to more popular beaches to the south; consequently, diving at Deer Creek Road can be uncrowded and rewarding.

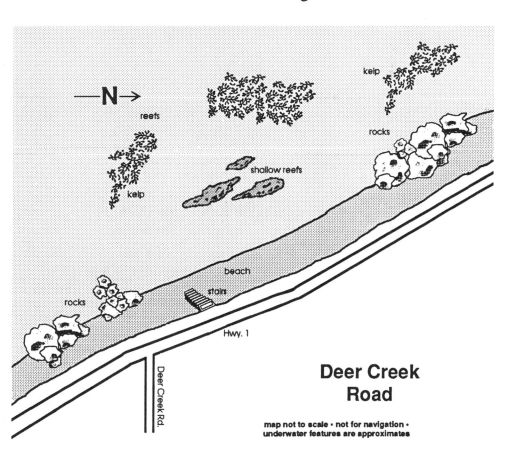

Deer Creek Road

map not to scale · not for navigation · underwater features are approximates

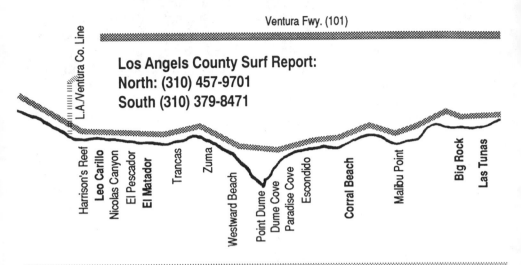

Map not to scale • not for navigation

Ventura Fwy. (101)

L.A./Ventura Co. Line

**Los Angels County Surf Report:
North: (310) 457-9701
South (310) 379-8471**

Harrison's Reef
Leo Carillo
Nicolas Canyon
El Pescador
El Matador
Trancas
Zuma
Westward Beach
Point Dume
Dume Cove
Paradise Cove
Escondido
Corral Beach
Malibu Point
Big Rock
Las Tunas

Introduction to
Los Angeles County

From the Ventura/Los Angeles County line, kelp beds become increasingly more common indicating offshore reefs. About a quarter of a mile from the county line is Harrison's Reef. Lying 200 to 300 yards offshore, Harrison's Reef is a dive for those who don't mind the longer swim. This kelp bed blends into, and marks the beginning of the reefs that lie parallel to Leo Carrillo State Beach. Here the kelp comes to within 25 yards of the sandy shore but water is sometimes murky.

The best part of the park for diving is off Sequit Point and the adjacent cove to the south. Off Sequit Point, the bottom is varied with many tall reefs that support heathy kelp and much sealife. Because most of the bottom is rock, visibility is usually good as well.

Farther south, the kelp begins again at Nicolas Canyon. Access is good, but the swim to the kelp can be a little too long. Access at El Pescador Beach is not as good and the swim can still be long through dirty water. A lesser known but good spot is at El Matador Beach. Access is not as easy as at Leo Carrillo but is safe. Kelp comes to within a few yards of the beach. Underneath the kelp, farther out, is an interesting reef in moderately clean water. From here

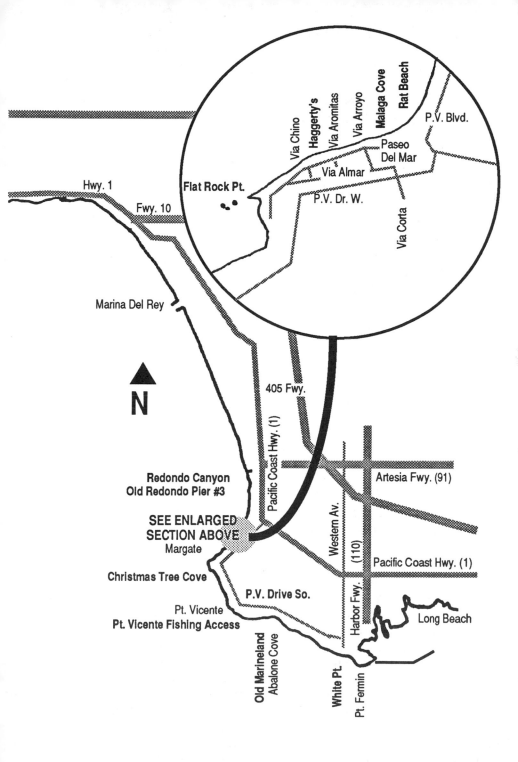

southward, there are many diving spots that are good but not consistently so. Trancas Beach is the next access point and is excellent for halibut hunting but little else. Zuma Beach, as well as Westward Beach, are fun dives with large sand dollar beds, pismo clams, and sometimes large surf.

Point Dume is excellent diving with a submarine canyon bringing clear water and much life but the dive is only for the experienced as treacherous currents can plague the area. Around the point, there is access to Dume Cove but visibility averages less than 10 feet. Little Dume offers similar conditions. Visibility in both these locations improve somewhat outside the kelp. Paradise Cove and Escondido Beach are also poor when it comes to clear water. There are some small but interesting reefs at Corral Beach which is frequently used by instructors as a spot for check-out dives. Visibility, however, is only fair.

Much of the Malibu coastline is difficult to access to due private property abutting the beaches. There are several access points in the Malibu Road area, just north of Malibu Point; but, visibility is poor, the beaches are open to high surf, and there is usually little to see on the sea bottom. Shore access, water clarity and reef structure improves somewhat beginning at the Big Rock Reef. Adjacent to Big Rock is Las Tunas Beach. Water clarity is better with some sea life, and an extensive reef area.

The Santa Monica Bay, or South Bay as locals call it, is a long, almost unbroken stretch of beautiful sand beaches. Interesting diving can sometimes be done due to some of the piers, but don't go in if prohibited. Artificial reefs present another alternative. All but one requires a boat to dive. There is a lesser-known artifical reef at 24th Street in Hermosa Beach that is within 200 yards of shore; there is, however, little left of it. A dive off the outside of the large Redondo Breakwater may reward you with some lobster, but heavy surge and a walk over large boulders can be a problem. Diving near the present-day pier or near the harbor mouth is prohibited.

Early in the century, a total of three piers were built off Redondo Beach for ships to take advantage of deep waters close to shore provided by the Redondo Submarine Canyon. The canyon comes very close to shore and makes for an interesting dive. The remains of Old Redondo Pier #3 can be seen today on the ocean floor off Topaz Street. At both the canyon and the old pier, visibility is usually good and the anemone-encrusted pier pilings make for interesting diving.

The sand beaches continue southward until Torrance Beach. Here, there is a little known reef out from the white cliffs at a place the locals call Rat Beach. Rat Beach and surrounding waters have long been noted as excellent halibut hunting grounds. The beach becomes much more rocky at the southward end of Torrance Beach where the shore turns westward to form Malaga Cove. This cove really marks the beginning of the excellent diving that the Palos Verdes area has to offer.

Palos Verdes is, unfortunately, also surrounded by cliffs making access to the water sometimes very difficult. At Malaga Cove there is good access on

a steep paved path and good diving over parallel reefs. Haggerty's to the west has more difficult access but better diving. Turning the corner at Flat Rock Point brings you even better diving but increasingly difficult access. Across Bluff or Paddleboard Cove is the cliff area known as Margate. Although there are some trails here, a boat is recommended. A few more coves southward is the small Christmas Tree Cove. Excellent diving in Palos Verdes' clearest water can be difficult to reach but usually worth it. Shore access from Christmas Tree to Point Vicente is spotty and dangerous at best. Around the corner is Point Vicente Fishing Access. Made infamous by "Cardiac Hill," the very steep and long but safe path leading to the water's edge, Point Vicente Fishing Access has some very good diving in nearby kelp.

Just recently opened to the public is the Old Marineland site. Shore access is easy, down gentle paths, and the diving is great. Shore access farther to the east becomes increasingly sparse. A very long walk will bring you to diving at Abalone Cove and at another point at Portugese Bend. Much of the diving in these areas can be in dirty water.

White Point is the only place around Palos Verdes where you can actually drive your car to the water's edge. You'll find a lot of divers at White Point but it's still an enjoyable excursion. A little over a half a mile down the road is shore access on the west side of Point Fermin where the water here is quite dirty. Cabrillo Beach near Los Angeles Harbor has good access but again poor water clarity. The harbor prevents any diving until you reach the sand beaches of Orange County.

Leo Carrillo/Sequit Point

One of the most prolific yet easily accessible kelp beds along the Southern California coastline lies as close as 20 yards off Leo Carrillo State Beach in west Los Angeles County. The shoreline runs east-west with two beaches being separated by rocky Sequit Point.

Sequit Point provides probably the best diving with kelp beds the size of several football fields. The reefs that stretch out from the rocky point support a wide variety of sealife. Many urchins, numerous species of starfish and anenomes as well as nudibranchs, mollusks, and small sponges attach themselves on the rocks under the kelp canopy. Photographers will enjoy the multitude of subjects available. Of particular note are the large number of colorful gorgonias that lie on the outer edges of the reefs.

For hunters, the rocks conceal a few small lobster, an occasional abalone, and rock scallops. The kelp cover attracts a wide variety of game fish including kelp bass and sheepshead. On the sand between the reefs, halibut is common.

Access to the beach west of the point and facilities at the park are not always available. Winter storms sometimes wash out the access road that leads directly to the beach to the west of Sequit Point. Recent brush fires have also taken their toll on the facilities. The positive effect of the road closure is the reduction in crowds. If the roads are open, there is a fee for day use and camping.

The best alternative is to park on the seaward side of the highway near the sign "Mulholland Hwy." This will place you within a short walking distance down a gentle slope to the entry-exit areas on the point.

Immediately to the west of lifeguard tower #2 and to the east of tower #3 are stairs that lead to sandy coves between the rocks that are excellent for entry or exit. The large kelp beds are easily visible running in as close as 20 yards to as much as a quarter mile out. Rips and currents can be unpredictable so observe conditions carefully. During the summer and on some holidays, lifeguards are present; it is wise to check with them.

There are some rocks in the surf, but careful observation before entry should prevent any problems. The bottom drops off moderately with kelp growing in as little as 10 feet of water. Although the kelp is abundant, it is not so thick as to prevent underwater passage in most locations. On the bottom, the reefs rise up as much as 10 feet in spots. An occasional tall boulder can be found usually covered with a wide variety of feather worms, anenomes, and other colorful invertebrates.

The diving area at Leo Carrillo is large. Because of this, alternate dive spots and entry/exit points can be found on the beaches on either side of the point. Each of these beaches face the ocean differently, thus giving you a number of diving options. It would take several dives just to begin exploring all the diving this area has to offer.

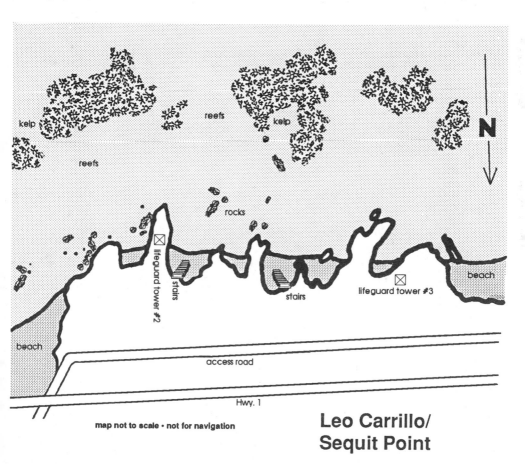

Leo Carrillo/
Sequit Point

El Matador

Quite a few divers are already familiar with the good beach diving that northwest Los Angeles County has to offer. Most of this diving activity is concentrated in the Leo Carrillo State Beach area which is understandable because Leo Carrillo offers good diving with a variety of underwater scenery and activities. What's not as well known by divers is that good diving can also be done nearby with fewer crowds and often better game. To the south of Leo Carrillo is a string of beaches, most of which are also part of the state beach system. They include Nicolas Canyon (not a state beach), El Pescador, La Piedra, and El Matador.

El Matador State Beach is the farthest south of these beaches. Although shore access and facilities are not as good as at Leo Carrillo, this beach offers some very good diving. Healthy kelp comes within 100 feet of shore. Rocky reefs extend out from the beach 150 yards with most of the reefs consisting of very large boulders on a sand and rock bottom. Several of these boulders rise from the bottom as much as 15 feet.

Attached to the boulders are bunches of gorgonian, corynactis, and giant keyhole limpets. Although this may not be the photographer's and sightseer's paradise, there is ample color and life here to fill the eye. Garibaldi, senoritas, and even a few bluebanded gobies dart about.

The hunter will find sheepshead, rockfish and kelp bass. On the sand surrounding the reefs, an occasional halibut can be seen. Although the size of the game fish in this area is not particularly big, the quantity is sufficient. Lobster are present in the right cracks and, unlike most of the Malibu area, abalone are also found in limited numbers. Look close for scallops, they are there also.

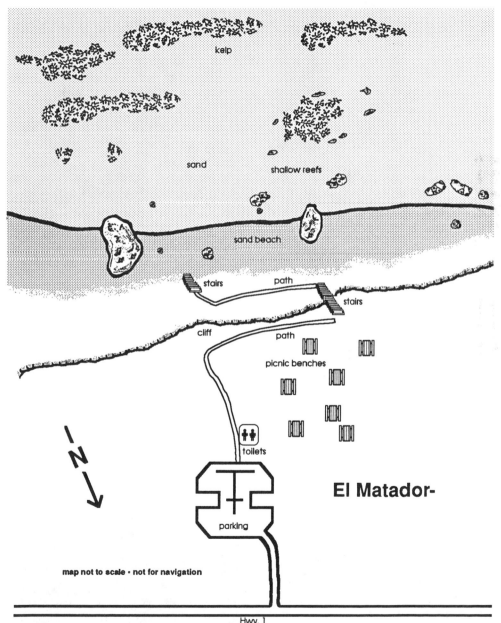

Conditions at El Matador State beach are variable because the beach is open to the weather. A day or two of pounding surf or rain will reduce the visiblity at the beach considerably, but on good days visiblity averages 10 to 15 feet. Occasionally, it reaches 30 feet in calm winter conditions or during Santa Ana winds. Currents are not much of a problem and usually only affect the outer edges of the kelp.

Locating the state beach is easy: The turn off to the parking area is directly off Pacific Coast Highway (Highway 1). The beach is approximately four miles south along the coast from Leo Carillo and two miles north of Trancas Beach. The turnoff is well marked with signs along the highway.

There is ample parking, chemical toilets and picnic benches. No overnight camping is allowed and the park is open from 8 a.m. to sunset. There is a day-use fee which is paid by using a self-service box on the side wall of the toilets. There is no running water.

The path to the beach begins at the toilets. The path is only moderately steep and is safe. The path is broken up by two sections of stairs for a total of about 80 steps.

Before descending the steps, take a good look at the beach. The first thing you will notice is the beauty of the beach. You may want to consider this beach for a picnic—with or without diving. Almost directly off the beach is a reef with rocks breaking the surface extending out about 75 yards. Depth on this reef runs between 10 to 20 feet. Although healthy kelp grows here, the visibility can be reduced due to surge. Snorkeling is also good when the surf is low. Looking out past the shallower reefs, you will see an additional bed of kelp extending 75 to 150 yards out. These reefs hold the best diving with depths ranging between 25 and 35 feet. In addition, there are large kelp beds extending along the shoreline in both directions creating a huge diving area that should satisfy everybody.

Corral Beach

Corral Beach is a simple, easy dive. Local instructors have used this location for years as a check-out dive spot for their students and although easy, it is an enjoyable dive as well.

This quiet sandy beach is located in the Malibu area of Los Angeles County, being passed frequently by divers from Los Angeles on the way up to more popular spots like Leo Carrillo State Beach. More precisely, Corral Beach is located about 2 1/2 miles east of Paradise Cove. Corral beach is popular in the summer with beach - goers and is sometimes crowded. On the extreme west end of the beach, out 30 to 75 yards, are small patches of kelp that reveal the location of submerged reefs and a good diving area.

Park just across from the Beaurivage Restaurant at 26035 Pacific

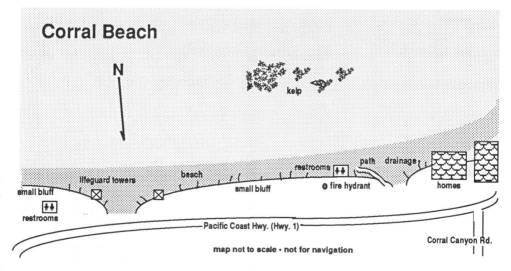

Corral Beach

N

kelp

lifeguard towers

beach

small bluff

restrooms

path drainage

small bluff

fire hydrant

homes

small bluff

restrooms

Pacific Coast Hwy. (Hwy. 1)

Corral Canyon Rd.

map not to scale · not for navigation

Coast Highway, using caution to avoid the no-parking zones and fire hydrant. At this point on a small bluff above the beach, ocean conditions can be observed carefully. There is also an easy path to the beach here.

Water entry from the beach is usually easy; however, a southerly swell, common in the summer, can create large breakers. Calm days in the winter or spring is usually the best time to dive this location. Out from the beach, the bottom drops off quickly to a rocky 10 to 15 foot deep bottom. This shallow area near shore is relatively barren but an occasional large boulder can produce a lobster.

The kelp closest to shore grows from some kind of man-made metal grid, origin unknown. Slightly further out is the bulk of the kelp growing from scattered boulders and small reefs. The largest boulder stands nearly 12-feet high and is covered with corynactis, gorgonia and a host of other creatures. On this and surrounding rocks, nudibranchs and starfish can be seen lazily grazing. The fish around this small reef is abundant as well. The orange garibaldi is fiercely territorial and stakes his claim in several sections. Some species of rockfish as well as kelp bass and perch, are present in sufficient quantities for fair spearfishing.

The spearfishermen may also want to cruise over the vast sand bottom in search of halibut. Other than the aforementioned fish for spearing, the hunter will not find much to bag at Corral Beach. The few rocks support almost no scallops and, although there are some good cracks for lobster, bug hunting is largely a hit or miss proposition.

If you choose to take your camera to this spot, it would be best to use a macro lens. Visibility is limited at best, averaging only five to ten feet. The poor visibility owes itself to two factors at this location: First is the creek drainage nearby, so avoid this location after heavy rains; Second is the beach's protected position from water-cleaning currents. Due to Latigo Point to the west, very little clean ocean currents reach the small reefs to carry away accumulated sediment.

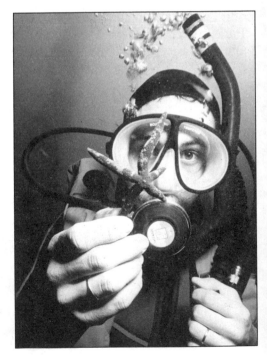

If you do not mind a little dirty water and are looking for an easy dive, Corral Beach may be an interesting spot to check out on your next beach dive outing.

Big Rock

Malibu is known for its recluse stars and celebrities with much of its coastline taken up with private beach bungalows and mansions. Beach access is often difficult with the large amount of private property abutting the beach but it can be done; you need to know exactly where to look for public water access. Several of these out-of-the- way shore access points lead to large healthy kelp beds with wonderful beach diving.

A large block of private beach front residences abuts on the beach known to locals as Big Rock. Just up the beach from the more popular Las Tunas Beach, kelp beds at Big Rock are often admired from afar by divers who think there is no access to the beach. Just off the 20000 block of Pacific Coast Highway, however, is a small public access way that is easy to drive past even when you are looking for it. The small gate opens to a few steps leading to a rock and sand beach fronting on an extensive and healthy kelp bed. Although the water entry can be tough, the diving is great and, although certainly not virgin, relatively untouched.

Big Rock gains its name from the medium large rock pinnacle inside the surf zone. A road just east of the beach access also gains its name from the pinnacle. Most local divers use this pinnacle as the jumping- off point for great kelp diving.

The beach is a peculiar mix of rock and sand. Depending on the time of year, the tides, and storm conditions, the face and shape of the beach can vary dramatically. Rocky beach surf entry experience is a must for diving this location. There are several large and small boulders in the surf so you must pick and choose entry and exit points carefully.

Also take time to study the surf. As previously stated, most divers choose to use "Big Rock" for protected entries and exits. Look for surge channels so that you may be pulled out over the reefs. The rock affords a number of points that offer some protection from small to moderate surf. Because of the large number of rocks and reef in the surf zone, this beach is best avoided when the surf reaches three feet or more.

Once out past the shallow reefs close to shore, the bottom drops away to 10 feet deep. Spot reefs support prolific growths of eel grass and, out a little deeper, feather boa kelp. Heading out farther, the bottom becomes mostly sand 15 to 20 feet down. At about 70 yards out, the giant kelp growth begins over large boulders and low-lying reefs. These close-in reefs are good areas to hunt for halibut but little else as the surge tends to stir up the bottom making visibility poor.

The best reef for sightseeing and other hunting begins about 100 yards out in 25 feet of water. An extensive reef structure is crisscrossed with crevices and large stands of healthy kelp. Look under large boulders for an occasional lobster or moray eel. Across the rocks are tiny pink anemones and rock scallop here and there. Small stands of golden gorgonia color the the bottom terrain.

Fish are plentiful with opaleye and perch being the most common. Up among the kelp fronds, spearfishermen will find calico bass to stalk. Other fish worth stalking at this site include halibut usually found in the sand surrounding the kelp beds.

Water exits must be as cautious as water entries. Careful planning before the dive is a must. Have a primary and secondary exit sights planned in advance. Before passing back through the surf zone, time the wave sets carefully and exit on a lull between waves.

Those looking for the comforts of home at this dive sight had better forget it. There are no facilities here. The nearest public restrooms are over a mile away to the north or south. Parking here is poor as well. There is only one public parking space directly in front of the access gate. More parking is available on the opposite side of Highway 1 making crossing the highway in full dive gear the most hazardous part of the dive!

Although it's perfectly legal to dive here (daylight hours only), private property surrounds the beach. Do not trespass and respect the permanent resident's privacy and quiet. By the way, don't be surprised if you are greeted by angry dogs as you walk on the beach. It's just another hazard of diving!

Las Tunas

Sometimes you just need a "quickie"! San Diego divers have La Jolla and Orange County Divers have Laguna Beach. Los Angeles divers have Palos Verdes and Malibu. The nearest major kelp beds for the heavily populated West Los Angeles, Santa Monica and San Fernando Valley areas are off Malibu. Heading west out of L.A. along Pacific Coast Highway (Highway 1), the first major kelp bed you come to with easy public access is at Las Tunas Beach. As it's only a few minutes drive from the end of Sunset Boulevard, this is a great spot for a "quickie."

But let's back up a minute and define a "quickie." So many California divers take for granted the

excellent diving we have right along our coastline. For many of us, we're only minutes away from spectacular kelp diving. Of course it's not quite as good as diving the Channel Islands, but consider the fact that you can have an exciting, stimulating dive in the morning hours before work or during a long lunch hour.

Rather than a dip in the hot tub after work, take a couple hours for a colorful dive along the coastline. With the long daylight hours of summer, you an easily get in a beach dive or two after work. And an added bonus is that dives can be made for only a few dollars for gas, air fill, and perhaps parking.

At Las Tunas Beach there is no parking fee. Parking is along the dirt shoulder on the ocean side of Pacific Coast Highway. Access to the water is only a few easy steps down a small bluff. Pause for a moment to first look over the conditions. The two-acre beach has a number of access points and beach faces.

In 1929, an erosion control program extended several metal and concrete groins into the surf designed to prevent sand from flowing away from the beach. The remains of those groins stand today as corroded and sharp submerged obstructions. Note their locations and use caution. The groins now only partially do their job and the face of the beach varies depending on location.

Several spots are narrow sandy beaches while surf crashes on barren slippery rock in others. The small sand beaches are the best for water entry. The bottom drops off quickly to a depth of 10 to 15 feet so the surf hitting the beach is frequently a sharp shore break. Surf, however, is generally not a problem. The most popular water entry points for divers are on the extreme east end of the

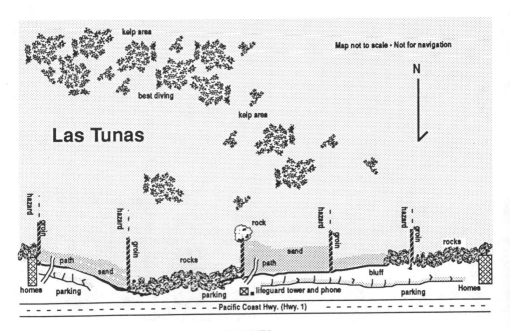

beach or near the middle next to the large rock directly out from the single lifeguard tower. The lifeguard tower is manned only during the summer and there is a phone nearby. There are, however, no other facilities.

Take a few moments before descending to the beach to look over the conditions. Time the wave sets. Even a small wave with a sharp shore break can slap you silly. Time your entry accordingly between wave sets and between waves. Also note carefully the location of the metal groins and make plans to stay clear of them during water entry and exit. This is also a popular beach for surf fisherman. Try to stay clear to avoid fishing line and hooks in the water. Be courteous and give everybody a chance to share the beach.

An extensive kelp bed extends from within 50 yards of shore to over 200 yards out. The kelp growth is healthy and quite thick in places. Although the kelp extends in close to shore, this shallow area offers poor visibility and little life.

At about 100 yards out, in the middle of the kelp bed, the rocky bottom becomes much more interesting and varied, providing habitat for a wide variety of life. Groves of golden gorgonia are common. Adding to the splashes of color are patches of corynactis anemones and an occasional sea lemon or Spanish shawl nudibranchs. Other interesting reef creatures to be found here include sheep crabs, sea hares, feather duster worms and an unusual number of octopus.

For other photo opportunities raise the camera up into the kelp. Las Tunas seems to be unusually plentiful with fish. Schools of large perch and grunts

cruise in and out of the cloudy waters. Large opaleye are also common and señoritas are plentiful. Don't come looking here for the bright orange garibaldi as they are curiously lacking. Up among the kelp fronds the sharp-eyed observer will spot the beautiful kelp fish as it blends into its surroundings.

While this is by no means a photographer's heaven, the underwater shutterbug will find enough subject material to perhaps justify dragging a camera through the surf.

The biggest deterrent to the underwater photographer is the visibility. Water visibility is only fair averaging only 10 feet in the shoreward side of the kelp. It does improve somewhat to as much as 15 or 20 feet on the outer kelp edges but this is too long of a swim for many divers.

Hunters, on the other hand, will definitely enjoy this location. Sand and kelp bass are bountiful, large, and relatively easy to approach. Halibut hunting is also good. The large flat fish can be spotted in the sand and gravel close to shore near the kelp stands. Lobster are present but not common. Most of the lobster inhabit the outer reef. Scallops are also present but again not in plentiful numbers.

Be aware that this beach can become quite crowded on summer afternoons. The best time to dive here is in the early mornings because of the better conditions and lack of crowds. If Las Tunas is "blown out," odds are so will all of Malibu and it would be best to check out Palos Verdes next.

If you live or work in the western half of Los Angeles County and have either a long lunch hour to kill, a weekend morning, or a need to escape the city tensions one summer evening, go to Las Tunas beach in Malibu for that "quickie."

Redondo Submarine Canyon

Along the Southern California coastline there are five submarine canyons that come close enough to shore to dive them from the beach. They are, from north to south, Hueneme, Dume, Redondo, Newport and La Jolla. Although not the most spectacular of the submarine canyons (that honor is owed to the La Jolla Canyon), the Redondo Canyon has probably the easiest access, shortest swim and best conditons.

Submarine canyons are a curious oceanographic phenomena. They are deep cuts into the continental shelf that transport ever shifting sands to the deep ocean floor and bring cold clear deep waters close to shore. Unusual marine life can be found in abundance in these canyons and Redondo is no exception.

Perhaps the most curious and interesting marine fauna that congregates here is the spawning squid that invade the deep trench in February and March.

Moving in at night, the massive schools of deep water squid rise to within just feet of the surface to spawn and lay their eggs. Clusters of the egg cases can be found spread out across the sloping mud bottom like bouquets of snowy white flowers.

The squid also bring in predators. Blue sharks, huge schools of bonita and seals are often seen while diving in the canyon during this special time of year.

Another curious occurrence is the congregation of decorator crabs. These interesting crustaceans vary in size from about the size of a golf ball up to six

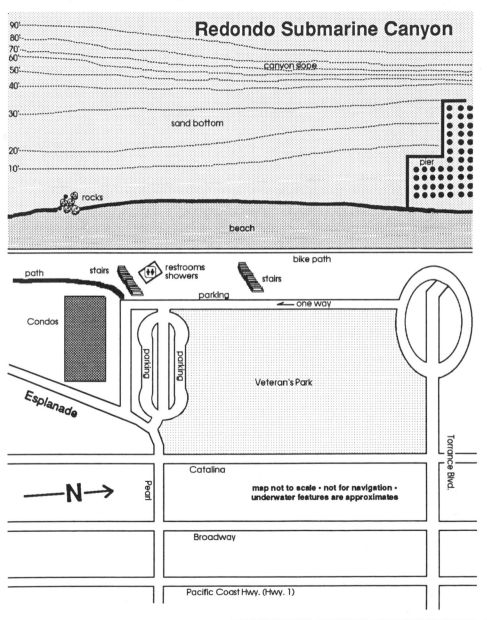

inches across. They get their name from their habit of camouflaging themselves by placing and growing a garden of algae on their shells. Also during the spring, hundreds of decorator crabs invade the canyon and group in piles of 10 to 50 in some sort of mating orgy. They appear as dark moving clumps on the bottom until you approach them; then, they break up and scatter in a matter that is somewhat humorous. The similar looking but larger sheep crab have also been reported to exhibit the same behavior in the area.

Marine life that can be found year round in and around the canyon include sea pens, sand stars, sea pansies, sand dollars, sea hares, octopus, halibut and a huge variety of snails.

The easiest dive into the canyon is launched from the beach off Veteran's Park, just to the south of Redondo King Harbor and pier. To reach the park, head west on Torrance Boulevard and turn left on Catalina Avenue. At the intersection of Esplanade and Catalina, just south of the Elks Club and Veteran's Park, is the parking lot; turn right on Esplanade and then into the lot. There is plenty of metered parking to the south and west of Veteran's Park. Don't forget to bring quarters for the meters. Try to arrive early as the lot fills up quickly especially in the summer.

Steps to the beach are at the west end of the lot. At the base of the steps are restrooms and showers. The edge of the canyon lies parallel to shore about 75 yards out. Directly off the steps is as good as any place to start your dive.

After a short walk across the sand, entry is usually easy if the surf is down. Because of the canyon, surf at this location will average two feet smaller than surrounding areas. The beach is an excellent choice during summer as southerly swells are blocked by the Palos Verdes Peninsula. Winter westerly swells can hit hard at times but are often interspersed with many days of calm water.

Swim directly out until you are about even with the end of the pier to the north. This will line you up near the lip of the canyon in about 35 feet of water. Drop down and head out to sea. Within a few feet the bottom will begin to drop away rapidly. If you have never made a canyon dive, nothing beats the thrill of looking into the dark mouth of a deep canyon.

The canyon drops rapidly to about 70 feet and then moderately to greater depths. Farther to the north, the canyon walls are slightly steeper and drop to as much as 90 feet before tapering off. It's very easy to find yourself in over 100 feet of water, so watch your depth. Stay well to the south of the pier as it is illegal to dive anywhere nearby. Beyond the pier is Redondo Harbor. Boat traffic can be a problem at times; hence, a flag and float is recommended.

Unfortunately, in recent years, this has become a very crowded dive site. The usually low surf conditions draw classes to the beach so you may have to wade through students floundering in the surf to get to the canyon edge. On the good side, few instructors take their classes into the canyon; consequently, the depths of the gorge are usually uncrowded.

But that's not to say the bottom of the canyon is untouched by man. The proximity of the canyon to busy beaches, pier and harbor has left the canyon scattered with human debris. Bottles, old and new, along with other trash, is common. Much of it provides homes for various marine life including octopus and bottom-dwelling fish. In the late 1980s, the pier to the north was heavily damaged by storms and then by fire. Some of the debris from this disaster can be found in the canyon. Around the turn of the century, a total of three piers stood off the beach—one directly off the south side of Veteran's Park (then the luxury Redondo Hotel). Destroyed by storm in 1915, the remains were explored by divers at the edge of the canyon for years until, in the late 1980s, storms and shifting sands all but erased the final evidence of the pier's existence. Only the submerged pilings to the south between Topaz and Sapphire remain (see dive spot "Old Redondo Pier #3).

Old Redondo Pier #3

Around the turn of the century, Redondo Beach was the hub of Los Angeles' maritime trade. The deep offshore submarine canyon, Redondo Canyon, allowed merchant ships to approach shore fairly close in calm seas. In the late 19th century, piers were erected off the beach to service the growing merchant trade. Items carried on the ships included lumber from the Pacific Northwest and goods from the Far East. It was a prosperous time for that section of the coast. Much of it became a resort for Angelenos seeking a holiday from the daily worries of big-city living.

Eventually, a total of three piers was servicing the shipping business. Pier #1 stood at Emerald Street, long since replaced, (several times) by the now famous Horseshoe Pier (itself heavily damaged by storms and fire in the late 1980s). Pier #1 was destroyed by a storm in 1914. At Ainsworth Court, next to Veteran's Park (then the luxurious Redondo Hotel) was the Y-shaped Pier #2. Reaching into the edge of the canyon, the pier was heavily damaged by a storm in 1915 and eventually was torn down, never to be rebuilt. The few underwater remains of Pier #2, just over the lip of the Redondo Canyon, disappeared in the late 1980s with winter storms.

The 480-foot long Pier #3, located between Sapphire and Topaz Streets, was also destroyed by a storm in 1926. From that time forward, the shipping boom for Redondo Beach was over as the new port at San Pedro was being constructed.

Pier #3 was the most prosperous of the three piers serving Redondo Beach and Los Angeles early in the century. The railroad ran to the length of the pier carrying cargo to and from merchant ships. The Pacific Steamship Company had a restaurant on the end of the pier as well. The storm of 1926 took much of that structure to the sea floor. Today, the only evidence of the pier's existence lies underwater.

The remaining pilings, numbering over 20, are the main attraction of this dive spot. Jutting up from the bottom as high as twelve feet, they are covered with beautiful pink anemones which make excellent

photo subjects.

Another attraction of this site are the artifacts that can be found on the bottom. Old bricks and broken dishes from the old restaurant are common. If you are lucky, you may find a bottle or a large piece of dish with an insignia.

The diving area can be reached by turning west on either Sapphire or Topaz off Pacific Coast Hwy. (Highway 1) in Redondo Beach. Both of these streets end at the Esplanade. Parking is along the street and access to the beach is via a pathway between the buildings at both locations.

The entry area is just to the north of the jetty. Facilities are good with showers at the lifeguard tower near the jetty and at the restrooms at the base of the path that leads to Sapphire Street.

Water entry is generally easy in light to moderate surf. The sand bottom slopes gently to approximatly 35 feet deep 100 yards out. It is here that remnants of the pier pilings can first be spotted. The best practice to locate the pier is to swim on the surface outward from the beach to just beyond the jetty. You should be directly out from the second set of condominiums just to the north of the jetty. Many divers locate the wreckage by swimming northwest across the bottom at a 45-degree angle from the end of the jetty. In any event, don't give up quickly. The pier area is long and narrow, and it is very easy to be either too far north, south, or too close to shore.

The area containing the most artifacts is closer to shore and is identified by the bricks scattered on the bottom. Digging in the sand here will produce broken fragments of dishes. The broken pilings are short and often covered with stalks of kelp. Depending on the weather, the kelp may reach the surface in some locations thus assisting the location of the dive site.

The tall pilings are seaward and more toward the north on the edge of the Redondo Canyon in about 40 to 45 feet of water. The Redondo Canyon begins to drop off moderately just to the north. If, in your search, you find yourself dropping into the canyon, you are too far north. Head up the sloping bottom to the south to find the pilings. The pilings are generally 15 to 25 feet apart or just out of visibility range, so move around to spot them all. The outermost pilings are about 200 yards out from shore.

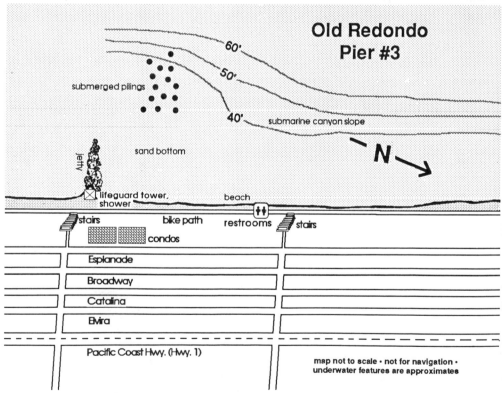

Old Redondo Pier #3

submerged pilings

60'
50'
40'

submarine canyon slope

sand bottom

jetty

N

lifeguard tower, shower

beach

stairs

bike path

restrooms

stairs

condos

Esplanade

Broadway

Catalina

Elvira

Pacific Coast Hwy. (Hwy. 1)

map not to scale · not for navigation · underwater features are approximates

Ocean conditions at this dive sight are generally good. Visibility is very consistent averaging between 10 and 20 feet. Upwelling from the nearby Redondo Canyon can increase visibility to the 30-foot range. Surf is little or no problem particularly during the summer months when the west-facing beach is well protected from the predominately south swell. Prevailing westerlies during the winter can occasionally bring big surf while any current is almost nonexistent. The only real persistent hazard is the boat traffic from nearby Redondo Beach King Harbor so a flag and float are recommended.

Hunting in the area is generally limited to good-sized halibut which are often taken in the sand surrounding the pilings. An occasional kelp bass can be spotted but is usually small. Sculpin or cabezon have been known to overrun the area from time to time.

Other sea life common around the pilings include the often comical but always slow-moving sheep crab. This member of the spider crab family can grow to be quite large, averaging 18 inches across and and as much as 24 inches. Octopus can be found cramped into small holes in the pilings, while on the sandy bottom, sea pens and sea pansies make their home.

Rat Beach

One of the most popular dive sites along the Palos Verdes Peninsula is Malaga Cove. This site is located along the Santa Monica Bay where the long, wide sandy beaches that are so famous in Los Angeles disappear into rocks and cliffs. It is also here that the beaches go from a north/south direction to a nearly westerly direction. What is created is a unique environment of kelp, sand and rocks which attracts an unusually bountiful variety of small sharks, rays, and other marine life.

Most divers hitting the waters of Malaga Cove head to the west and the lush kelp. But another, much less heavily visited site lies just 200 yards away off the sandy beach to the north. This beach is known by the locals as "Rat Beach."

The term "Rat Beach" has nothing to do with local wildlife but rather is an acronym for "Right After Torrance." A lot of people are unaware that Torrance even has a beach, which is a short stretch of sandy beach that extends from public parking, rest rooms and beach access in the north to just short of Malaga Cove on the south. What people call Rat Beach is really part of Torrance beach but is less frequented by the crowds.

The easiest access to Rat Beach is from Malaga Cove. Unknown to most divers, intermittent reefs in 15 to 20 feet of water extend from Malaga Cove northward to a major reef off Rat Beach. On days of exceptional water visibility, these reefs can be spotted from the gazebo on the bluff at Malaga Cove.

While the reefs off Rat Beach are not as interesting as those at Malaga Cove, the life in waters surrounding these rocks is often superior.

Bat rays are quite common and it is not unusual to see several on one dive. Frequently they can be quite large with wing spans of over five feet. When you find bat rays, halibut are almost sure to follow. The halibut like to hide in the sand near the low-lying reefs. If you move quietly through the water, you may also spot the shy leopard and sand sharks.

Over the rocks, the fish life is plentiful. Kelp and sand bass are common and exceptionally large. Other common species include opaleye, surfperch, and halfmoons.

Life on the rocks, on the other hand, is sparse. Kelp is even sparser and eel grass has trouble getting a hold on these rocks swept with surge.

The reefs here are shallow with depths running between 10-20 feet. Furthermore, the beach is exposed to a common westerly swell. All of this combines to create an environment that is intermittently swept with sand and brushed clean of all but the hardiest reef dwellers.

Visibility is poor, averaging 5 to 10 feet. But good days of visibility of 20 feet are frequent enough to consider this as an alternate dive site to Malaga Cove.

With the bountiful kelp bass, halibut and other fish, certainly this is a

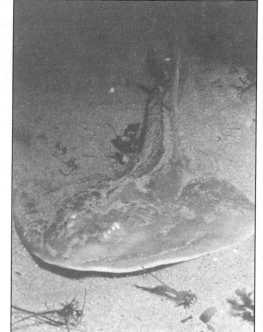

good site for the spearfisherman. While lacking in colorful reefs and clear water, you may think this to be a poor spot for the sightseer and photographer. Not so. The presence of huge bat rays makes this an exciting dive for all.

Jumping off point for this shore dive is the same for Malaga Cove. Pacific Coast Highway joins with Palos Verdes Drive West in South Torrance. Follow Palos Verdes Drive West into the town of Palos Verdes Estates; turn right at Via Corta and then right again at Via Arroyo. Cruise past Malaga Cove Elementary School and the parking for Malaga Cove is to the right of where Via Arroyo intersects with Paseo Del Mar.

There is adequate parking and a gazebo that overlooks the cove. From here if you train your eyes up the beach to the north, you will spot a large light-colored section of the bluffs jutting from the darker bluffs. It is directly out from these white bluffs that the Rat Beach reefs lie. If the water is clear that day, you may be able to spot the reefs from the gazebo. They will appear as a dark section of water 30 to 50 yards from shore.

A short steep path leads down to Malaga Cove from the parking lot. Water entry and getting to the reef can be done in one of two ways. The first option is to walk the 200-odd yards along the beach to the white bluffs, enter the water there, and swim directly to the reefs. Option two is to enter off the rocks at Malaga Cove and swim over, either by compass on scuba or with snorkel.

Swimming from Malaga Cove is recommended. The water off the rocks is frequently calmer and with scuba gear on your back, swimming is easier than

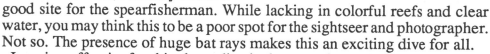

walking. Most importantly, however, you will enjoy the stroll underwater. Between Malaga Cove and the Rat Beach reefs are several small intermittent reefs running parallel to each other and perpendicular to shore. It is in the sand between these reefs you will often see bat rays and halibut.

Rat Beach is a further attraction simply because it is a beautiful beach. With no direct access, it is frequently uncrowded even on hot summer weekends. With the attraction of the old favorite, Malaga Cove, and the new site, Rat Beach, you may want to bring two tanks.

Malaga Cove

Malaga Cove lies where the long sweeping beaches of the Los Angeles South Bay end, and the rocks and cliffs of Palos Verdes begin. This makes for an interesting bottom offering sand, rock reefs and kelp beds.

In the rocky areas, lobster are not uncommon although most are not very big. Considering the good access to Malaga Cove, these waters hold a fair amount of game. Kelp bass can be found around the kelp beds and over the sand, halibut and angel sharks. For those that don't mind a longer swim, rock scallops can be found farther out. Some black abs are present but don't count

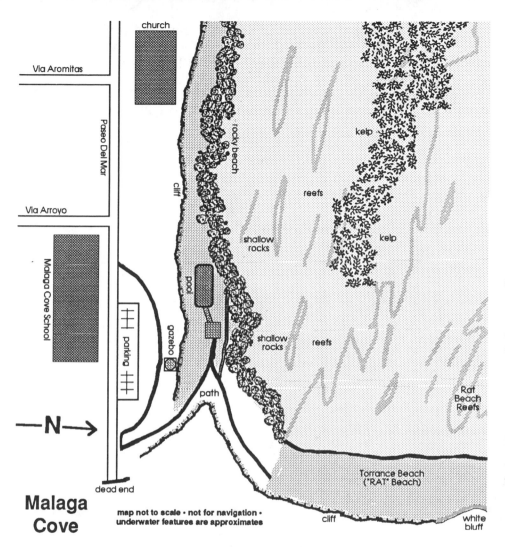

church

Via Aromitas

Paseo Del Mar

Via Arroyo

Malaga Cove School

parking

cliff

rocky beach

kelp

reefs

kelp

shallow rocks

pool

gazebo

shallow rocks

reefs

path

Rat Beach Reefs

—N→

dead end

Malaga Cove

Torrance Beach ("RAT" Beach)

map not to scale • not for navigation •
underwater features are approximates

cliff

white bluff

on coming here to fill your bag.

For the photographer and sightseer, diving Malaga Cove will show you marine life not easily found in other beach dive locations around Palos Verdes. Coming across an angel shark buried in the sand can be an exciting experience. Some divers have reported seeing some as large as five feet long. If you look closely in the rocks, you may find a horn shark or an octopus. The comical sheep crab often crawl across these rocks. You will also find the more common varieties of invertebrates, including colorful bat stars, ochre stars, nudibranchs, and gorgonian. Garibaldi are also abundant and quite tame.

To reach Malaga Cove, exit Pacific Coast Highway (Highway 1) in the city of Redondo Beach to southbound Palos Verdes Blvd. Palos Verdes Boulevard will pass through a portion of Torrance and then into Palos Verdes Estates. Here it will swing around to the east briefly and then to the west, passing in front of beautiful Malaga Cove Plaza. Here, turn right toward the sea on to Via Corta which will veer west, turning into Via Almar. Turn right again at Via Arroyo in front of Malaga Cove School. This will bring you to Paseo Del Mar. The parking area will be clearly visible to your right.

After parking, proceed to the gazebo that overlooks the cove from the cliff above. This vantage point is excellent for observing the ocean conditions below.

There is a paved path that leads to the beach off to the right. The path is moderately steep but short. If you have a cart, you can wheel your gear down to the beach and suit up there.

There are two general areas in which to enter the water: from the rocks adjacent and in front of the swimming pool or from the beach to the right. Entering from the rocks shortens the swim to the outer kelp considerably but can be hazardous in moderate to heavy surf. The area immediately in front of the rocks is quite shallow. High tide is the best time to enter from the rocks. Many divers prefer to enter at the sand beach and swim out to the edge of the reefs. If entering from the beach, watch out for surfers. Your choice will depend on your preference and the conditions at the time of your dive.

Although visibility averages 12 feet, conditions at the cove vary considerably. The cove is open to the westerly and northwesterly swells. When the weather is up from this direction, it is advisable to head to the other side of the peninsula. In addition, storm rain water run-off can affect the visibility. If the weather is coming from the south, or if a Santa Ana condition exists, Malaga cove can offer superb diving with visibility up to 25 feet.

After your dive, Torrance Beach, adjacent to the cove, offers a secluded sunning spot that is relativly uncrowded compared to the rest of the South Bay.

Haggerty's

Searching the coastline surrounding Palos Verdes for good shoreline access, we come to a spot known as Haggerty's. The location gets its name from a millionaire who used to call this area his home. The diving off Haggerty's is very good although the access can be difficult but not impossible.

The sea bottom here is relatively flat, made up of rock and low- lying reefs sloping gently to 35 feet on the outer edges of the kelp. The rock bottom supports a large, healthy kelp bed. The kelp is thick in a few spots but not enough to prevent passage by divers. The amount and variety of sea life found in the kelp beds is one of the largest in the Palos Verdes area.

Huge sheep crab is perhaps the most dominant form of life on these reefs. Their size, slow movements and inability to cope with persistently curious divers make them enjoyable to watch. They can reach up to two feet across and it is not unusual to see three or four in one dive. Sea hares or sea slugs are another readily available life form found under this kelp bed. Many are quite large reaching the size of soccer balls. Also look for the sea hare's clusters of yellow eggs.

Although there are more colorful sections around Palos Verdes, photographers will find plenty of material to keep them busy. The generally good visibility and strong kelp growth also make for good pictures.

Visibility at Haggerty's averages 15 feet. Winter storms and rain tend to play havoc with the water clarity but the summer and autumn months often hold

days of 20 to 25-foot visiblity. The area is relatively current-free. Surf can be a problem during westerly swells; however, good protection from southerly swells makes this spot a good choice for summer months.

Game is available in limited numbers. Both Malaga Cove and Haggerty's have long been consistent producers of lobster although not in large numbers. Looking closely may reveal an occasional abalone hiding under the rock ledges. Unlike the area south of Palos Verdes Point to Dana Point, abalone is legal to take here; however, local divers have a "gentleman's aggreement" not to take any abalone north of Palos Verdes Point to preserve and replenish their numbers.

Access to the Haggerty's dive site is less than a half mile southwest from the popular Malaga Cove dive spot. To reach this area, follow Pacific Coast

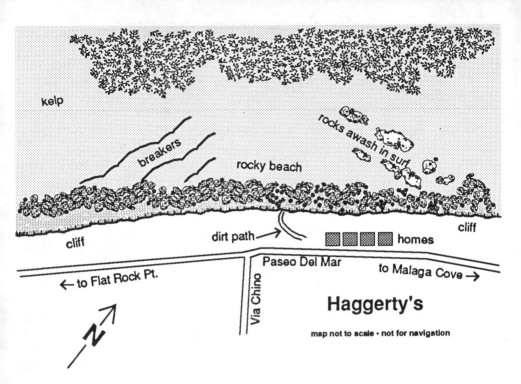

kelp

breakers

rocky beach

rocks awash in surf

cliff

dirt path →

homes

cliff

← to Flat Rock Pt.

Via Chino

Paseo Del Mar

to Malaga Cove →

Haggerty's

map not to scale · not for navigation

N

Highway (Highway 1) to the city of Torrance. Turn south on Palos Verdes Drive West and follow it into the city of Palos Verdes Estates. Across from Malaga Cove Plaza, turn right toward the sea at Via Corta. Via Corta will go down the hill then veer west, turning into Via Almar. At the first stop sign, turn right on Via Arroyo passing Malaga Cove Elementary School. At the intersection with Paseo del Mar, the parking lot above Malaga Cove (another good dive site) will appear to the right; however, here you will turn left. After passing Neighborhood Church on the right, park on the street at Via Chino. The path to the beach is over the small field and begins at the top of the bluff.

The path is short and steep. It is only for the sure-footed and must be taken slowly, particularly on the lower portion. In recent years, the last 10 feet or so of the path have suffered the effects of severe storms and has become very difficult to pass. A cooperative dive buddy can help by handing dive gear down to you. After a rain it is best to avoid this access because the path becomes loose, muddy and slippery. The top of the bluff offers an excellent vantage point to check out the surf, entry and exit points, and the conditions of the dive site below. Water entry is over the rocks. Should you find the path impassable, you may wish to dive Malaga Cove just down the road. Malaga Cove offers a paved access road.

Flat Rock

Many divers agree that the west side of Palos Verdes offers some of the best coastal diving in Southern California; however, much of it has poor or no access. Flat Rock Point, which does offer access to good diving, marks the location where the coastline around Palos Verdes swings to the south again.

Flat Rock Point offers excellent diving on an interesting sea bottom. The bottom drops off quickly from shore to a 25 to 35 foot bottom made of boulders and reefs that run in the pattern of ridges rising from the bottom 5 to 10 feet. Between the ridges, small patches of ivory sand create clearings in the forests of healthy kelp that seem to grow almost everywhere.

The lush kelp and excellent reef formation support an excellent variety of fish life. Numerous garibaldi, senoritas, kelp bass, sheepshead and other varieties are found here. The spearfisherman may be frustrated however; much of the gamefish varieties are on the small side with the possible exception of the large halibut that pass over the small sand patches between the reefs.

Flat Rock point has long been a consistent producer of lobster. Much of the near-shore reefs have been picked clean of the larger bugs; however, outer waters, and sometimes the very shallow waters, can produce a big bug. Abalone are slowly making a comeback due largely to a gentleman's

agreement to not take abs. Please respect that agreement.

The photgraphers and sightseers will enjoy the usually good visibility. Averaging 15 to 20 feet, the kelp beds are ideal for exploring the underwater forest-like surroundings. On the bottom, colorful nudibranchs, starfish, gorgonias and anemones make their home. Other invertebrates include an abundance of sea cucumbers, keyhole limpets, and sea hares. In the reef crevices, it is not unusual to find the yellow and black striped treefish, the small and shy bluebanded gobies or even an occasional horn shark. Urchins are common, so watch those knees!

Shore access to the point is difficult but not impossible. Flat Rock Point is located just down the road from other popular Palos Verdes dive spots such as Haggerty's and Malaga Cove. Proceed to the area via Pacific Coast Highway. In the city of Torrance, exit on Palos Verdes Blvd. proceeding south. Follow this road as it swings to the west into the town of Palos Verdes Estates and past beautiful Malaga Cove Plaza. Here you will turn right on Via Corta. Via Corta will turn into Via Almar as it swings to the left. After passing Via Arroyo, Via Aromitas and Via Media, you will come to Paseo Del Mar; turn left here. The head of the trail leading to Flat Fock Point will be directly ahead where the road rises sharply and begins to curve to the left at 600 Paseo Del Mar.

The trail to shore begins as an old dirt road (sorry, no vehicles). The trail then breaks off to a moderately steep, dirt path (avoid after a rain when the path will be muddy and very slippery; even when dry, the trail can be treacherous).

Proceed with caution.

The trail ends at the flat rocks (hence the name) on the point. Here, depending on the size and direction of the surf, entry is best made directly off the rock where it drops sharply to 12 feet of water or deeper. Experience in this type of entry/exit is important for shore diving this spot. There are also some small coves in the rocks to the northeast of the point that can be used if the surf is right.

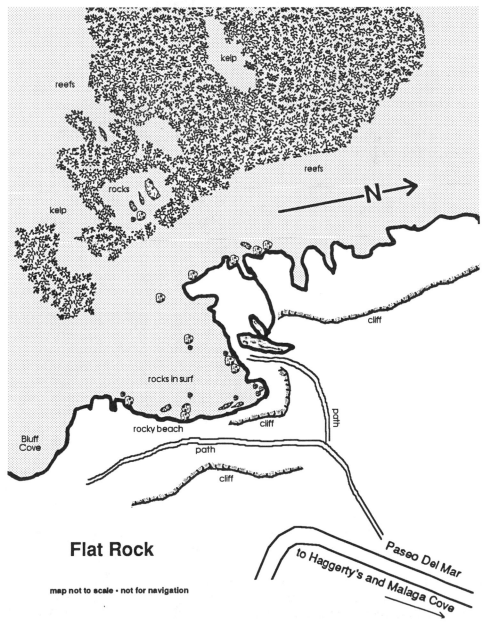

Flat Rock

map not to scale · not for navigation

Christmas Tree Cove

The reefs at Christmas Tree Cove are, in spots, quite spectacular. In one location, a large section of the reef, the size of a bus, juts 18 feet from the bottom and drops vertically to a kelp bed below. Other areas of the reef have overhangs, channels, and huge boulders. Surrounding the reefs are lush kelp beds. All of this is waiting to be explored in water that has the best visibility for the area. Averaging 15 to 25 feet, the visiblity here rarely drops below 10 feet and is frequently as much as 35 feet.

The thick, healthy kelp and rugged bottom terrain provides a habitat for a large variety of sea life. A wide selection of sponges, anenomes, and starfish make the rocks their home. Many mollusks are in residence here also. Varieties such as the giant keyhole limpet, wavy turban snail, kellet's whelk and shiny brown chestnut cowrie are easily found. Splashes of brilliant color are provided by the red and blue Spanish shawl and bright yellow sea lemon nudibranchs. Watch out for those knees; urchins seem to be everywhere. Swimming above and around the abundance of life on the reefs are opaleye, rock wrasse, the ever-friendly garibaldi, and seemingly hundreds of senoritas. In the crevices, the shy striped treefish resides and the tiny but colorful bluebanded goby darts about.

There is a good share in the game department also. Although not as plentiful

as in other areas off Palos Verdes, game fish in good numbers are present here. In the sand that surrounds some of the kelp, halibut is occasionally present. Also in the kelp and on the rocks are kelp bass, sheepshead and, in fewer numbers, rockfish. Scallops and lobster are also present but in limited numbers. Keep in mind, however, that abalone is illegal to take in this area.

The biggest setback of this dive spot is the poor shore access which is via a steep dirt path along the north side of the cove. The path is for the sure-footed and stout-at-heart. In some spots, particularly after rain, the path can be hazardous.

The top of the path can be reached by proceeding south on Palos Verdes Drive West off Pacific Coast Highway (Highway. 1). Drive through the town of Palos Verdes Estates for roughly five miles and turn west on Paseo Lunado. This will turn into Paseo Del Mar as it swings along the coast. The foot of the

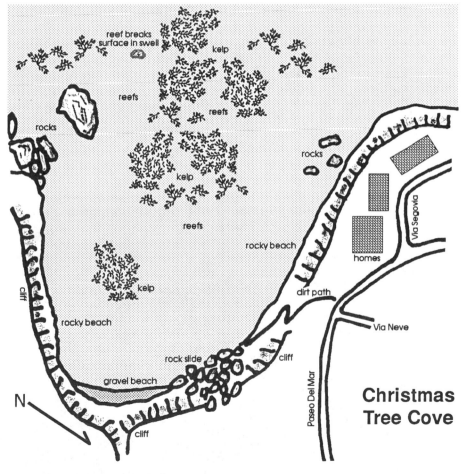

map not to scale · not for navigation

path is located at the 2800 block of Paseo Del Mar, near the intersection with Via Neve. There is limited but usually ample parking along the street. There are no facilities.

Ocean conditions can be easily observed from the top of the bluff. After proceeding down the steep trail, water entry can be made through the surf at the stone and gravel beach in the center of the cove or, if conditions permit, over the rocks on either side of the cove. It is a long swim through thick kelp to reach the best reefs on the outer edges of the kelp. There are, however, interesting reefs and kelp beds closer to shore.

If conditions are poor elswhere, Christmas Tree Cove usually holds the best possibility for good diving.

Point Vicente Fishing Access

Diving around Palos Verdes is excellent but shore access can be very poor. Divers take what they can get and one of these shore access points is the Point Vicente Fishing Access, aptly nicknamed by locals as "Cardiac Hill." Luckily, however, it's not as bad as it sounds.

The steep trail is located just to the west of the Point Vicente lighthouse where Marineland, now empty and abandoned, is almost a stone's throw away. There is good parking and restrooms with a drinking fountain at the top of the trail. The trail, or Cardiac Hill, is long and steep but fairly safe. Diving along the shoreline at the bottom of the hill is worth the effort.

The beach between Point Vicente and Long Point (where Old Marineland is located) is fairly large offering a wide diving area; however, the best location is to the east at the end of the branch trail that heads toward a small rocky point. The east branch trail is a little narrow in spots but visibility is usually best here and, depending on conditions, entries are usually best here as well.

Entries are over rocks and are sometimes difficult. The sandy beach in the center of the cove offers possible easy entry and exit but requires a longer walk and longer swim to the clearer waters to the east. Before descending the trail, determine the conditions and your diving goals to best choose the areas where you wish to dive and also where to enter and exit the water.

The bottom drops off at a moderate slope reaching as much as 50 feet within 150 yards of shore where it begins to level out to sand. Most of the reefs consists of boulders of varying sizes; some are very large and extend to within ten feet of the surface creating large caves and overhangs that are exciting to explore. These large boulders can sometimes be spotted from the cliff top when water visibility permits.

Visibility here is fair, averaging 10 to 15 feet. Once again, it is usually best on the east side of the cove which is somewhat protected from northwest swells and weather, but open to south swells during the summer. The bottom is covered with much silt that can ruin the water clarity in times of heavy surf. Close to shore, strong currents are usually not a problem, but near Point Vicente, currents have been known to reach two knots.

On the rocks, life is not as abundant as in other areas around Palos Verdes but there is certainly enough to see, photograph and hunt. Invertebrates calling this area home include giant keyhole limpets, nudibranchs, and, on the ledges and overhangs, corynactis anemones. For color, look for the small but numerous stands of gorgonia in the deeper water. Sea hares and sea cucumbers are also common in the deeper waters. Fish life includes garibaldi, senoritas, and for the hunter, opaleye and an occasional halibut on the sand. Hunters will also find a few scallops and lobster. This is an abalone moritorium area; taking them is illegal here. Kelp cover on the reefs is hit and miss. If the kelp growth is heavy, you can expect more game moving in the cove.

Old Marineland

Here, dolphin and man swam together. You could dive with hundreds of sharks in relative safety and snorkel among colorful reef fish. But, due to an act of man, this is no more. Was it a massive ecological disaster? A mass killing? No, this was the act of real estate developers.

For over 30 years, California's oldest theme park sat along the coast on the Palos Verdes Peninsula. It entertained thousands with its fantastic exhibits of marine life that were years ahead of its time. Perhaps more importantly, they inspired thousands of youngsters into further exploration of the ocean realm.

A few short years ago, under circumstances that some say were scandalous, Marineland was bought, its animals removed, and much of it torn down. It was then sold again. The site's ultimate fate is still up in the air. Initially, it was to have been a convention hotel; then a resort hotel; now, there is talk of real estate development.

One thing very positive has come out of all the confusion. The present owners of the land, the Monahan Company, have seen fit to make the shoreline open for public access. Divers now have a new, wonderful dive site they can explore on beach dives.

The original builders of Marineland were smart folks. They wanted a site that acted as a continuance of what was inside the tanks. They wanted a site

of pristine oceanic beauty. In Southern California, perhaps one of the most beautiful stretches of coastline is along the Palos Verdes Peninsula. They chose Long Point. The point extends far into the clear waters of the San Pedro Channel and marine life is abundant. During the winter and spring, gray whales can be seen migrating just offshore. Seals haul out on the rocks. The kelp is thick and fish are plentiful.

While we certainly cannot return to the days of the 50s, much of this section of coastline is still unchanged. The kelp, seals, whales and fish remain; only now, divers have easy access to the location.

With all the great diving that exists along the Palos Verdes Peninsula, its one drawback has always been the poor and limited access to the shoreline. Along the entire peninsula coast, there are only a couple of easy accesses to the shore. The opening of the old Marineland site to the public is a welcome event.

Sure it's great to have a new beach dive site, but more importantly, this is truly a great beach dive! The coast here runs approximately from east to west and is somewhat protected from the prevailing west to northwest winds and seas.

At this location, there are two points where gentle, easy paths lead to water's edge. To the east, an old paved road (pedestrians only, please) leads to a small cove with a cobble stone beach. To the west, a dirt road and path leads to the point where a rocky beach surf entry is possible. In between these two points are about 300 yards of rocky reefs, kelp forests and great diving. There is also an extensive reef and kelp system to the west of the point and a hidden reef out from the cove.

Those choosing to enter and exit the water from the point must have rocky beach surf entry experience. There are a number of places to enter and/or exit the water depending on the tides. Find a good spot with a somewhat flat rock near the water line to put on your fins. Look for a surge channel between two rocks. As a swell pushes water up to a high level, enter the water. Push off the rock and the receding surge will pull you out away from the surf zone. A reverse of this technique will bring you in, washing you up on the rock with the incoming swell.

While this technique is easy to learn, it does take some practice under the eye of an instructor experienced in rocky beach diving. This technique is also easier for entries than with exits. An excellent dive plan for this site is to enter off the rocks at the point (assuming you know how), take a compass heading, and head underwater for the cove, exiting the water there. Divers with less experience may want to enter and exit the water at the cove. Watch your footing on the cobble stone beach as the smooth stones can be slippery and hazardous.

From shore, the bottom drops off rapidly to 15 or 20 feet. Kelp is fairly close to shore in 20 to 30 feet of water. The rocky bottom continues to drop away at a moderate rate to between 35 and 50 feet where a gently sloping sand bottom takes over 50 to 75 yards from shore. The bottom tends to drop away quicker and deeper, closer to the point. The cove is mostly sand bottom with scattered boulders and reefs. Farther to the east from the cove is a rocky point that extends underwater as a rocky reef. Out from the cove, across the sand bottom, is another rocky reef about 75 to 100 yards out.

The varied depth, rocky reefs, kelp forest and sand bottom make up an interesting underwater terrain that is rarely boring. In the shallows are patches of eel grass, ribbon kelp and a lot of urchins. The kelp forest near the point is full of fish. Look for the bright orange garibaldi as they dart in and about the rocks and kelp strands. The garibaldi are less friendly here than at other more popular dive sites as they're probably not yet used to divers that are always willing to give a handout of food.

On the other hand, hunters will be pleased on how easy it is to approach such favored game fish as calico bass, sheephead, and sand bass. Although scallops are common, some being quite large, lobster seem to be rare in spite of the excellent habitat of jumbled boulders. Abalone are non existent and are illegal to take here as this dive site falls in the abalone moratorium area covering from Palos Verdes down to south of Dana Point in Orange County.

The rocky reef is highly varied with crevices, large boulders and ridges that rise as much as 15 feet from the bottom. Sand pockets and channels break up the bottom that is rarely the same in any two places.

Out from the kelp is probably the most interesting portion of the dive. As the kelp disappears, gorgonia takes over. In the deeper (40 to 50 feet) portions of the reef, large stands of golden gorgonia cover the boulders. As the boulders taper off into the sand, tube anemones become abundant and large.

Don't stop at the sand. Frequently buried in the sand near the reef's edge are large Pacific Electric or "torpedo" rays. Although sightings of these fascinating creatures are rare in Southern California, they seem to be common at this location. A torpedo ray with a wing span of nearly three feet across was reported on one recent dive.

A word of warning: Look but don't touch! Torpedo rays have the capacity of electric shock and will deliver a powerful blow if provoked. Also be aware that these creatures are not afraid of human beings. They have been known to aggressively pursue divers.

Other interesting creatures abiding along the edge of the reef include octopus (often quite large); a variety of starfish in a number of shapes, sizes and colors; and colorful nudibranchs.

In shallower waters, 6 to 30 feet down, you may find what remains of the Civil War era ship known as the *Newbern*. On October 13, 1895, the wood hulled, steam powered vessel ran aground in thick fog and subsequently broke up on the rocks. Although most of the $250,000 cargo of silver bars was recovered, two 25-pound ingots remain missing to this day. For divers, all that remains now are an occasional piece of brass, rotting wood hull, or corroded iron spikes. The remaining debris from the wreck lies just east of the point.

To reach the old Marineland dive site, take Palos Verdes Drive South to the old entrance to Marineland. The sign looks much the same as it did years ago but minus the whale and dolphin sculptures. The large blue sign reads "Monahan Company, Long Point." The road will take you to the parking lot.

Head for the far end, near the old park entrance next to the tower still standing. The road to the water's edge begins here but no motor vehicle traffic is allowed beyond this point. The access is open from 8:00 a.m. to 4:00 p.m. Please note the sign at the top of the hill. It reads: "Right to pass by permission and subject to control of owner," meaning the access can be revoked at any time. Please respect the fact that this is private property. Let's not give them a reason to restrict access. There is no fee for parking but there are also no facilities.

Years ago the show at Marineland was in tanks on dry land. The show is still here, you just have to get wet to see it. That makes it more fun anyway.

White Point

The only location along the Palos Verdes Peninsula where the public can drive right down to the water's edge is White Point. Thousands of divers have had their first underwater experience here and although this location is noted as being a "beginner" dive spot, divers of all levels will find something of interest.

Perhaps what makes this spot interesting to all is the same reason there are ruins here. Before World War II, the local Japanese-American population built a bathhouse here over natural hot water vents. The ruins can still be seen just above the high-tide line, but most of the hot water vents are only visible to the diver. There is no other spot like it along the coast.

The vents are located in the rocky bottom very close to shore, the nearest being less than 25 yards out. They are easily spotted by the strange white fungus growth that surrounds them. This fungus growth is supported by the vents. On some of the larger vents, the warm water can actually be seen and felt rising from the rocks. Do you get cold hands? Run your fingers through the warm sands at the vents. These oddities make very interesting study.

Diving in the surrounding area is, quite frankly, only average for abundant and beautiful Palos Verdes. That is not to say it is poor; on the contrary, it is comparatively good.

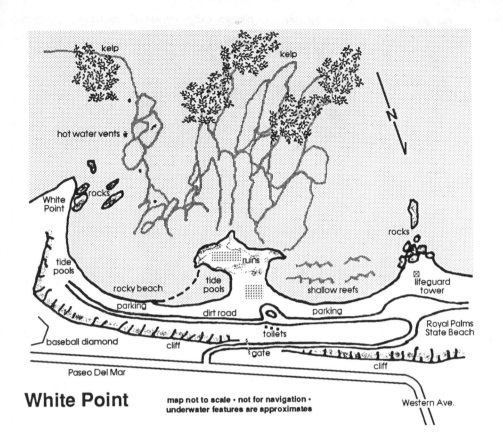

kelp
kelp
N
hot water vents
rocks
White Point
tide pools
rocks
ruins
tide pools
rocky beach
shallow reefs
lifeguard tower
parking
dirt road
parking
Royal Palms State Beach
baseball diamond
toilets
cliff
gate
cliff
Paseo Del Mar

White Point

map not to scale · not for navigation · underwater features are approximates

Western Ave.

The water in the tiny bay is shallow and covered with many urchins. The shallow area is good for beginning snorkelers when the water is calm. Beyond this, there are reefs that extend off the points to the north and south. All of the reefs are quite interesting with many overhangs, crevices and small caves. Farther out, some 150 to 200 yards, three reefs extend out parallel to each other separated by sand. Covered by 35 to 45 feet of water, it is here that the best diving is found. The offshore reefs are, however, best left to the more experienced diver because of the longer swim and frequent currents.

On and in the reefs are starfish, including the colorful bat star, ocre star and many nudibranchs, particularly the beautiful orange and blue Spanish shawl nudibranch. Other invertebrates to be found here include a variety of anemones, sea cucumbers, giant keyhole limpets, and, in deeper waters, gorgonian. There was, at one time, an underwater nature trail but heavy storms in recent years have all but wiped it out. There are plans to rebuild it. A new plaque was recently installed in the center of the cove commemorating the site's long diving history (Japanese abalone divers first began exploring these waters around the turn of the century). For the photographer, there are also some morays but surprisingly few garibaldi.

Hunting is poor from years of pressure from the divers; however, some species are returning. Lobster can be found on the deeper reefs. Abalone, particularly the black abalone, is making a slow comeback but this one is a definite NO-NO. White Point lies in the abalone moritorium area: Do not take! Spearfisherman will do fair on the deeper reefs with some sheepshead, halibut and kelp bass. In shallower water you'll find some perch and many opaleye.

In 1932, the ferry *Melrose* wrecked on the point and broke up. Subsequent storms further broke the wreck into tiny pieces and spread them over a wide area. If you are lucky, small bits, including brass nails, and small other items can still be found.

Conditions at White Point are usually good. Visibility on the reefs

averages 10 to 15 feet. The deeper offshore reefs can be somewhat better. The small cove where most divers enter is somewhat protected but can be hazardous, particularly on the rocks at high tide. As previously stated, currents are often present on the outer reefs.

Reaching White Point and adjacent Royal Palms State Beach is quite simple. Proceeding south along Western Avenue, through the town of San Pedro, will bring you to the top of the cliffs overlooking the sea where Western Avenue will swing left joining with Paseo Del Mar. The road to the point is less than one block down the road at 1800 W. Paseo Del Mar. It is the only road to the sea in the area and, although unmarked, it is hard to miss. Depending on the time of year or time of day there is sometimes a day-use fee for the state park (Royal Palms).

Pause for a moment at the top of the bluff before paying the fee to enter. The view from the bluff is excellent and a brief overview will determine ocean conditions. Take note of the hours posted at the gate. The gate is closed and locked promptly at the posted closing time, trapping any tardy cars. If conditions look good, proceed down the hill and bear left all the way until the road turns to dirt. Another 100 feet or so of driving will bring you to the small cove which most divers use for entry, only a few steps from water's edge. Park off to the side. Extensive renovations are planned for this area in the near future so the roads and facilities may change.

Some divers choose to enter off the rocks at either point but this is best left for the very experienced. Water entry in the small cove is over small boulders that, at times, can be hard on the feet. Entry as well as exit can be a little

difficult but is eased by the area's usually small surf. Again, entry or exit at high tide can be difficult due to swirling currents in the shallow water and around the rocks.

Introduction to Orange County

Perhaps the most concentrated area with excellent beach diving locations is the southern Orange County coastline. From the Los Angeles County line to the southern side of the mouth of Newport Harbor, diving is generally limited to sandy bottoms or under piers, where permitted. When the surf is down, diving under the Newport Pier can be very interesting as the pier reaches to the lip of the Newport Submarine Canyon.

Just south of the mouth of the Newport Harbor is the beach at Corona del Mar. Diving here is shallow on rocks to the south, or on the Newport Harbor breakwater. An occasional lobster can be found in these rocks. The next small beach down the coast is known as Little Corona. The small cove at Little Corona is flanked on both sides by rocky reefs that make for interesting underwater exploration.

Past the town of Corona Del Mar is Crystal Cove State Beach. Having recently undergone extensive renovation, the facilities here are now excellent. There are several good shore access points in the park but the one that leads to the best diving is at Reef Point (a.k.a. Scotchman's Cove).

Heading southward into the town of Laguna Beach, one finds the largest concentration of beach diving spots. Starting with Cresent Bay, diving is good but the best is a very long swim away to the offshore Deadman's Reef. The next cove over is the famous Shaw's Cove. Although generally crowded with divers, this beach dive spot is not to be missed.

Equally spectacular and much less crowded is the diving off the small Fisherman's Cove. One hundred yards to the south and within the ecological preserve is Diver's Cove. From Diver's Cove, the coastline stretches out into a small sandy beach known as Picnic Beach. Picnic Beach offers excellent facilities and good easy diving in offshore kelp. Rocky Beach uses the same facilities but entries are slightly more difficult over the rocks. Diving is, however, just as good if not better. The excellent reefs off the point at Rocky Beach can also be accessed from Main Beach near the center of town.

Reefs thin out and hang farther offshore directly in front of Main Beach. Heading southward, the kelp is thick and there are many good access points and dive sites. The access at Cress Street leads to exceptional diving over a rocky bottom covered with kelp. Small coves such as Woods Cove or at Moss Street are more protected from the weather and offer excellent reef formations close to shore.

South of these small coves, the water clarity begins to deteriorate. Victoria Beach has good access down some stairs but water clarity is not consistent.

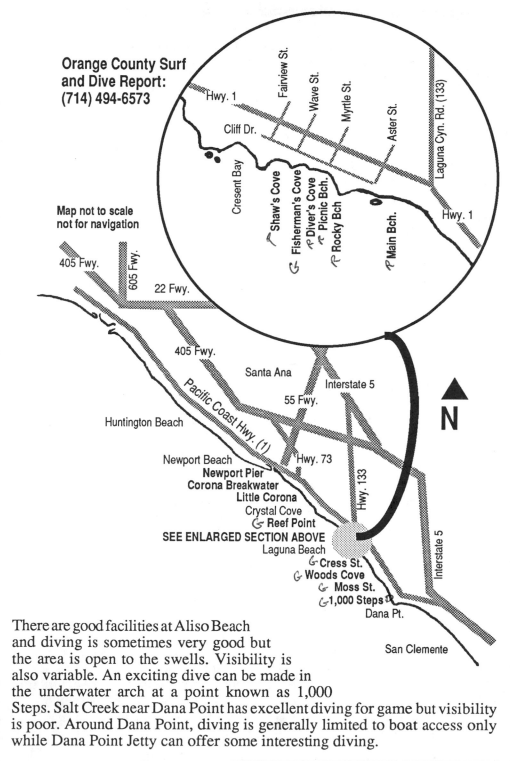

Orange County Surf and Dive Report: (714) 494-6573

Hwy. 1

Fairview St.
Wave St.
Myrtle St.
Aster St.
Laguna Cyn. Rd. (133)

Cliff Dr.

Cresent Bay

Map not to scale not for navigation

Shaw's Cove
Fisherman's Cove
Diver's Cove
Picnic Bch.
Rocky Bch

Main Bch.

Hwy. 1

405 Fwy.
605 Fwy.
22 Fwy.
405 Fwy.

Santa Ana

Interstate 5

55 Fwy.

Pacific Coast Hwy. (1)

Huntington Beach

Newport Beach
Newport Pier
Corona Breakwater
Little Corona
Crystal Cove
Reef Point

Hwy. 73

Hwy. 133

Interstate 5

N

SEE ENLARGED SECTION ABOVE

Laguna Beach
Cress St.
Woods Cove
Moss St.
1,000 Steps

Dana Pt.

San Clemente

There are good facilities at Aliso Beach and diving is sometimes very good but the area is open to the swells. Visibility is also variable. An exciting dive can be made in the underwater arch at a point known as 1,000 Steps. Salt Creek near Dana Point has excellent diving for game but visibility is poor. Around Dana Point, diving is generally limited to boat access only while Dana Point Jetty can offer some interesting diving.

Newport Pier

There are many piers along our coastline which attract abundant sea life but most also extend out over very gently sloping sand planes. Consequently, water depths at the end of the piers are seldom deeper than 20 feet. Diving conditions are usually poor with much surge and limited visibility. The Newport Pier is an exception.

The Newport Pier is a man-made structure that has turned a barren sand flat into homes for literally dozens of species. This unique spot is filled with sea life not usually found within a pier structure. Making this spot unique is the Newport Submarine Canyon that begins where the pier leaves off. Where most piers reach a maximum depth of 20 feet, the Newport Pier has a full depth range from shore to nearly 40 feet at the end.

Entry is easiest to the North of the pier as this is the area closest to the main parking lot. Parking is plentiful with meters so bring lots of quarters.

As you make your water entry, watch out for the fishing dory boats that launch through the surf. As soon as you're past the breakers, head into the pier and do your actual snorkeling within the pier structure. Fisherman do not normally relish the idea of divers interfering with their pastime, so be cautious during your entry and snorkel to the pier.

Once you've reached the halfway point begin your decent, but don't head for the bottom immediately. Pick a piling and see how much and who lives there. Mussels are large and have thickly overgrown the piling. Any number of giant green anemones or strawberry anemones can be found tucked in and around where the mussels have grown. Octopus can be seen in the crevices, no doubt a perfect spot to watch and wait to feast upon the crabs congregating along the sand bottom. On the sand, small slender crabs (*Cancer gracilis*) are most commonly found in two's, procreating their species. These slender crabs, small enough to fit in the palm of your hand, are often mistaken for the juvenile dungeness crab. So many scatter the ocean floor that once two exposed crabs are disturbed and swim off, you'll notice two more slightly buried under the same spot that the previous two just left. Use caution if you look for crabs beneath the surface of the sand; you may come across a thornback ray commonly found here on the sand flats they call home.

Surf perch are found, typically in shallow water, and very small groups are often found on the opposite side of the pier that the fisherman frequent. Large schools of mackerel and sardines can be seen swimming between the pilings in and out, over and over again, making for great schooling fish photos. If you can't get that photo the first time, wait a few seconds and the school will turn around and zig-zag through once more. Not too frequently seen is the California barracuda. It can be spotted within the pier pilings for a brief moment before it takes off for open ocean.

As you inspect each piling and work your way toward the end of the pier, it all begins to look like a "who's who of the ocean world." Not only do you encounter life commonly found on offshore reefs, you also get a chance to see, up close, the sand and bottom dwellers you usually bypass on your way out to offshore kelp.

Towards the end of the pier, the bottom will take on a very gradual slope reaching as much as 40 feet in depth. At the bottom of the pilings you'll find piles of starfish—literally starfish on top of starfish on top of starfish. Look closely at this conglomeration and you'll see ochre stars, short spined stars and even giant spined stars. All of these stars belong to the the *Pisaster* family, the most common large starfish group along the Southern California coastline. The ochre star is the most striking for photographs in this location. The vibrant purple, red, orange and yellow colors stacked one on top of the other couldn't have looked more staged even if you tried. The photo opportunities are great. Many of the stars are of gigantic proportions owed no doubt to the abundant mussels they feast upon that reside on the pier pilings.

As you look at the marine life on the bottom at the end of the pier, look out to open ocean and notice the bottom terrain. It's not an optical illusion you're seeing; the bottom *is* tilting. Actually it's a moderate slope which marks the beginning of the submarine canyon off Newport Beach. Only five locations off the Southern California coast have submarine canyons close enough to shore for beach diving: Hueneme, Dume, Redondo, Newport and La Jolla.

While you may be tempted to head off into the canyon, heavy boat traffic and

abundant active fishing lines make it not worth the risk. The canyon has gently sloping walls when compared to the canyon dives at La Jolla, Redondo or Dume; consequently, the venture into the canyon is not as interesting as the marine life around the pier.

As you explore the bottom, you will come across evidence of man's long presence at this site. Commonly lost or thrown off the end of the pier are knives, fishing poles, money, pistols, bottles, bicycles and more. The pier has been around for over a century and was once a center of commerce where ships tied directly to the pier and a railroad reached out to greet them. Very old coins and bottles still occasionally turn up.

Once you reach the end of the pier and make the turn to go back, make sure you stay within the pier structure. Fishing line and tackle litters the perimeter of the pier and is quite heavy at the end. The buddy team is at its best when watching for fishing line. Make sure you do dive with a good knife, even the most careful eye can't always spot the sometimes invisible monofillament line.

Across the sand, in depth ranges from 10 to 20 feet, you may find the elusive pismo clam. Prized for their good eating, divers can skim across a surgy sand bottom in search of the delicacies. In this part of the state, the size limit is 4 1/2 inches at the shell's widest point, the limit is 10, the season is open year round, and you must have a current California sport fishing licence.

Other than the pismo clams, underwater hunting here is poor. You may find an occasional game fish out near the end of the pier such as a halibut; otherwise, it is best to leave the gun at home. There are some rock scallops on the pilings but concerns about pollution tainting should ward you off.

Underwater photographers will do better than the hunters. There is a lot of unusual life both on the pilings and in the sand. Macro photographers will do great with abundant subject material on the pilings. If the visibility is good, the pilings make a great back drop for wide angle work.

Water conditions at the site are variable. Visibility averages five to 15 feet. The pier's proximity to the submarine canyon does, however, improve water clarity somewhat. The beach where the pier is located faces southwest; consequently, it is open to winter storms from the west and heavy south swells that occasionally come in the summer. Surf can be a problem. Call the surf report for conditions before heading for the site. If the surf is three feet or more, plan a dive elsewhere.

After the dive, there are freshwater showers on the beach just north of the pier and restrooms at the base of the pier. There are many great restaurants and beach-side food stands within walking distance or you may just wish to spend some time in the sun on the beautiful beach adjacent to the pier.

Corona Breakwater

Breakwaters are an excellent habitat for lobster. Warm waters from inland bays and harbors bathe the rocks and supply the crustaceans with a great deal of food in the form of decaying organic matter. Harbor breakwaters are generally made up of large boulders jumbled on a sand bottom. This creates large crevices, small caves and a "condominium" for lobster. Many breakwaters, however, have limited or no access or are constantly being pounded by surf. The Newport Bay harbor breakwater at Corona Del Mar State Beach is an exception.

This breakwater is located on the southeast entrance of the Newport Bay harbor. It is approximately 300 yards long and made up of jumbled rocks and boulders lying on a sand bottom from 15 to 35 feet deep. Two things make this a very good dive site: lobster and the surface facilities.

Although lobster are available at this location, don't expect to bring home your bag limit. What makes this an attractive lobster hunting spot is its easy access. Being a state park, the location is fully developed with the parking lot right on the beach. One has only to don his gear, make a few steps across the beach, and you are at water's edge. If you like, to save a little swimming time, you can walk out across the breakwater and slip in over the rocks.

On the beach are showers, lifeguards, fire pits, picnic tables and restrooms.

Sand is a problem easily remedied either with the showers or by dressing and undressing on the parking lot pavement or small grassy areas nearby. There is even a seasonal snack bar. Because this is a state beach, however, there is a day use fee payable at the gate. It would be wise to take a few minutes to observe beach conditions from the street nearby, on the bluff, before investing the fee.

Conditions at the breakwater are usually good. The one very obvious exception is when large swells are coming in from the south as is often the case in the summer and early fall. When calm, visibility at the breakwater averages 15 feet. Surge is common but usually tolerable. Call dive reports and use Laguna Beach as a reference.

Lobster is not the only catch on the breakwater. Game hunters will also find sheephead, rockfish, and halibut on the sand in the late spring and summer months. Abalone is illegal to take here. Photographers will enjoy the gorgonia, garibaldi, starfish, and other invertebrates. Although the photographer will find colorful life here, the sightseer will do better to the south in Laguna Beach.

This is a fairly safe place to dive but you must be aware of at least one hazard. Due to its proximity to the Newport Bay harbor, the location does get a fair amount of boat, water ski and jet ski traffic. Although a dive flag is not required, using one may be wise.

If you wish to make a day of it, bring a second tank and dive the southeast side of the cove; here you will find shallow reefs covered with eel grass and other sea life. The entire area is also excellent for snorkeling on calm days at high tide or incoming tide.

To reach the breakwater, head for the Corona Del Mar area of Newport Beach in Orange County. In Corona Del Mar, turn off Coast Highway at Marguerite Avenue. This will bring you close to the entrance of the beach park. The breakwater is to the right.

Little Corona

Experienced divers often shy away from the more crowded dive spots thinking that great diving must lie in some remote location below sheer cliffs. In some cases this is simply not true. One of these fine, yet often crowded, dive spots is Little Corona.

Located in the southern corner of Newport Beach, less than a mile south of the mouth of Newport Harbor, Little Corona gets its fair share of summertime crowds, but divers keep coming back.

Perhaps the biggest reason for this dive spot's popularity is that it rarely fails to surprise. At any given time, large halibut can be found in the sand or a four-

foot horn shark can be seen cruising these reefs. Although the area has been worked over by divers for many years, lobster, kelp bass and rockfish are still in residence.

While the reefs to the south, off Laguna Beach, tend to be more colorful and livelier, Little Corona has a good supply of sightseeing and photo subject matter. On the reefs, in water 20 feet and deeper, small gorgonians, starfish, feather-worms and different varieties of other invertebrates can be found.

Visibility here is generally good. Water clarity on the outer reefs can reach 30 feet, but the visibility usually averages 15 feet. Nearer to shore, the visibility can drop due to water turbulence over the sand but is usually good enough over the shallow reefs for snorkeling in calm weather.

Little Corona can be easily reached by turning south on to narrow Poppy

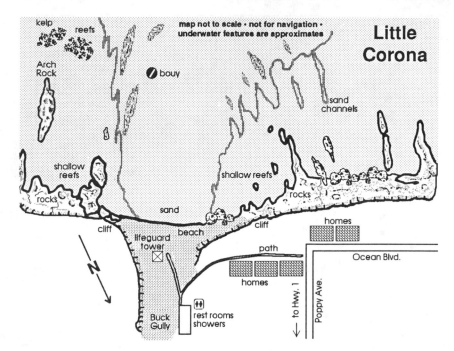

map not to scale · not for navigation · underwater features are approximates

kelp
reefs
Arch Rock
buoy
sand channels
shallow reefs
shallow reefs
rocks
rocks
sand
cliff
beach
cliff
homes
lifeguard tower
path
Ocean Blvd.
homes
to Hwy. 1
Poppy Ave.
N
Buck Gully
rest rooms showers

Street off East Coast Highway (Highway 1) in Newport Beach. Poppy Street will end overlooking the sea and turn sharply on to Ocean Boulevard. There is very limited free parking on Ocean Blvd; the path to Little Corona is just to the left of this intersection. A paved, moderately steep path winds down to the beach. From the top of the path, sea conditions can be easily observed. Half way down the path, tucked in a corner to the left, are restrooms and showers.

On the beach is a lifeguard tower that is manned on busy summer days. The lifeguards do discourage spearfishing because of the crowds. If you would like to spearfish, dive during a less crowded time.

The reefs start very shallow and, near shore, drop on a moderate slope to 30 feet deep 150 yards out. The shallow reefs are often covered by a thick growth of eel grass. The middle of the cove is mostly sand but there are numerous small rocks in the surf line that can trip you up in entry and

exit. The reefs lie on either side of the sandy cove with the most interesting ones to the south and out about 100 yards. Note that there is a buoy in this area that directs boats to stay clear. Several interesting reefs lie just outward and to the south of this buoy. Further down the coast is the interesting Arch Rock that rises from the water and is usually inhabited by several birds.

Although the buoy directs boats to stay clear, it is always a good idea to use a flag and float in this location due to its proximity to Newport Harbor.

Keep in mind that this is a part of the Newport Beach Marine Life refuge. It is illegal to take any marine life other than normal game. Check the specific regulation posted along the path that leads to the beach.

Reef Point
(a.k.a. Scotchman's Cove)

In the short history of sport diving, this dive site looms large for game hunting. Old-time divers know this site as Scotchman's Cove but recent renovations to this section of Crystal Cove State Park has brought a new name to the dive site— Reef Point—as indicated by the sign posted on Highway 1.

This location has produced many world records as well as personal records for white sea bass, black sea bass and other game.

Although Reef Point does not produce the game it has in the past, many beach divers still find it a reliable spot for the hunting of all types of species. Lobster can still be found in water 30 feet or deeper and sometimes in the shallows among the eel grass. Scallops are also available but usually in outer waters and abalone are present in small numbers but illegal to take due to the moritorium. The best quarry seems to be the game fish. The most common are calico or kelp bass and sheepshead. Other varieties are available but most are very cautious due to the heavy spearfishing activity in the area.

Reef Point is also a delight for the underwater photographer and sightseer. There are large-reef structures that rise from the bottom as much as 20 feet in some locations. These create walls of rock on which gorgonia, starfish and anemones attach themselves. With the crevices, cracks, and overhangs, in addition to the patches of sand between the reefs, the varied bottom makes for interesting exploration. Growing from the rocks is ribbon kelp. The larger kelp beds are mostly gone, but may grow back in the near future.

Visibility is good. It averages between 10 and 15 feet but can reach 20 to 30 feet in the winter. The area is open to heavy surf and as a consequence, visibility can suffer during times of large swells.

Perhaps what makes Reef Point even more attractive are the excellent facilities recently installed on the bluff overlooking the beach. Reef Point lies in the southern end of Crystal Cove State Park. Much of the park has undergone renovation and improvement. There are new restrooms as well as freshwater showers and sinks. Several new paved parking spaces have also been added. An underwater nature trail is being planned for the near future. Because the cove lies within the state park, there is a fee charged at the gate.

To reach the gate at Reef Point, proceed along the Coast Highway (Highway 1) until just north of the town of Laguna Beach. The gate is indicated by the sign "Reef Point".

The path and stairs to the beach are just beyond the new restrooms on the bluff. The path is moderately steep but safe. Observation of the diving area is excellent from the bluff. A large reef extending from the point is located just up the coast to the right. Diving is good on both sides of the reef but weather, surf and currents will determine the best area in which to dive. Entry on the sand beach is through the surf. As previously stated, the area is open to the swell and is best avoided during periods of large surf.

The bottom drops off quickly to 10 to 20 feet. Several shallow reefs with much eel grass make this an excellent area for snorkeling during calm weather. The deeper and more interesting reefs lie 100 to 200 yards out. Try closer to the exposed offshore reef for best sightseeing and game.

Shaw's Cove

Shaw's Cove is one of the most frequented dive spots in Laguna Beach. Every weekend, it is not uncommon to see two or three classes using the cove for checkout dives and several buddy teams entering and exiting the water with smiling faces. Conditions here for beach diving come as close to being ideal as any other place along Laguna Beach. The crowds are perhaps the only drawback, but don't let the crowds stop you from diving this superb location.

The cove is well protected from wave action; consequently, the surf averages only one to two feet. Currents are weak or nonexistent and the visibility is rarely below 15 feet and often exceeds 35 feet.

Classes are conducted here for the excellent variety of instructional conditions. Students can be taught surf as well as rock entries and exits under mild conditions. Excellent snorkeling is available also.

The bottom terrain is both interesting and varied. On the western side of the cove, the rocks extending from the point drop rapidly to the sand in 20 to 35 feet of water. At the end of the point, there is a large channel 15 feet wide that starts in 20 feet of water and cuts deep into the reef. Divers that frequent the area call this "the crevice."

To locate the crevice, swim on the bottom along the edge of the rocks tward the sea. The crevice begins as a 15-foot-wide cut into the reef running approximately west. The

crevice then narrows to a tunnel or arch that is often filled with garibaldi and is a photographer's dream. The crevice then continues to branch off into smaller channels and tunnels; some of which hold octopus that can be hand fed. Be aware: surge can effect the area creating currents in the crevice. For the more experienced diver, this can be used to their advantage by allowing the surge to whip the diver in and out of the channels. During low tide, the underwater activities can be observed from the rocks on the surface directly above the crevice. Simply stated, diving the crevice can be just pure fun.

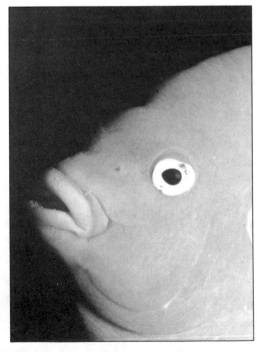

Farther out along this reef, the water deepens and sea life becomes even more abundant. Beginning in about 30 feet of water, large fans of gorgonia adorn the rocks. Garibldi become more abundant and are just as friendly. Adding to the color are nudibranchs and a variety of anemones.

Shaw's Cove is part of the Laguna Beach Marine Life Refuge which permits the taking of most game fish and lobster. Disturbing all other forms of aquatic life is prohibited.

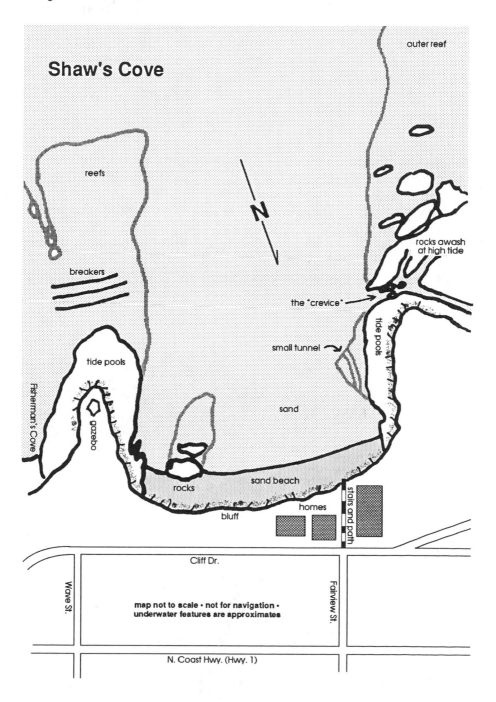

Shaw's Cove

outer reef

reefs

N

rocks awash at high tide

breakers

the "crevice"

small tunnel

tide pools

tide pools

Fisherman's Cove

gazebo

sand

sand beach

rocks

homes

stairs and path

bluff

Cliff Dr.

Wave St.

Fairview St.

map not to scale · not for navigation · underwater features are approximates

N. Coast Hwy. (Hwy. 1)

Game is sparse in Shaw's Cove, probably due to the frequency of divers. On the outer fringes of the reefs, an occasional morsel can be found.

Diving on the eastern side of the cove is less spectacular but far less crowded. A shallow reef covered with blade kelp and eel grass extends from the eastern point out about 100 yards ending in sand 25 feet down. This reef tops out at 10 to 15 feet and is excellent for snorkeling. At several points along the sand, the reef rises vertically from the bottom as much as eight feet. These mini-walls are inhabited by colorful gorgonia and anenomes. On the far side of the eastern reef, there is a shallow channel that is inhabited with a variety of fish and, in one particular crevice, two huge moray eels.

Shaw's Cove is located between two other favorite Laguna Beach dive spots: Crescent Bay to the north and the lesser known Fisherman's Cove to the south. A short walkway and stairs that lead to the cove are located at the end of Fairveiw at Cliff Drive, a block from North Coast Highway (Highway 1). Parking is on the street and is very limited. It is best to arrive early or go on weekdays. If nearby parking is full, deposit your gear and buddy at the top of the stair and park farther away to avoid a long walk with your equipment. The cove is surrounded by private property. Respect their privacy by keeping quiet and not trespassing.

A block south from Fairview at Wave Street and Highway 1 is a dive store if you'd like to fill your tank for a second dive and across the street is a burger stand to fill your belly.

Fisherman's Cove ✦
(a.k.a. Boat Canyon)

The majority of divers who descend upon Laguna Beach often choose Shaw's or Diver's Cove and for good reason. Some of the best beach dives that Orange County coast has to offer is found at these two locations. Although the dive spots are ideal, they do have their drawbacks: First, the everpresent crowds of eager divers; and second, the fact that Diver's Cove falls in a marine/ecological preserve and no game may be taken. Shaw's Cove has no normal game restrictions but is just about depleted due to its popularity. Smack dab between these two dive spots, less than 100 yards from both, is a relatively little-known spot called Fisherman's Cove.

Also known as Boat Canyon, due to the large number of catamarans found on the shore and in the small gully, the small cove falls within the Laguna Beach Marine Life Refuge. Here, the taking of normal game (see specific regulations) is permitted per Fish And Game Regulations. What makes this so important is that a good amount of game can be found at Fisherman's Cove—including lobster!

Directly in front of the small beach, about 75 yards, is a reef that breaks the surface with exposed rocks and extends shoreward to the southeast side of Fisherman's Cove. This reef is one of the more interesting in Laguna Beach. Many those diving from Diver's Cove end up here anyway. Approaching it from Fisherman's Cove is much easier. The reef rises from a sand bottom, and holds a number of deep channels, large crevices, and overhangs. Located in 25 feet of water less than 60 yards from shore, the channel is located on the shore side of the north edge of the reef. The channel varies in width from 10 to 20 feet, with walls as much as 15 feet high and cut with many crevices full of creatures. Farther out on the reef, the rock walls become quite steep rising from the bottom as much as 25 feet. A few feet to the north, across the sand, are some medium-sized patch reefs. On the seaward side of the reef and to the east, more channels and crevices can be found. In short, the reef at Fisherman's Cove is an excellent habitat for a wide variety of marine life.

Considering its proximity to the more frequented dive areas, Fisherman's Cove has a good amount of game. The cracks and wide crevices lend themselves nicely as homes for lobster. Although many are shorts, a good amount of legal sized bugs can be found here. Fair-sized sheepshead, kelp bass, and an occasional halibut in the sand will entice the spearfisherman. Even an occasional good-sized scallop or two can be found on the rocks, but sorry, no abalone. Besides, they'd be illegal to take anyway as the cove falls into the abalone moritoruim area.

One note of caution: The reef on the southeast end of Fisherman's Cove continues into the Diver's Cove area. As previously stated, Diver's Cove is part of a marine/ecological preserve in which the taking of game is prohibited. The boundary is marked by a crack in the point dividing Diver's Cove and Fisherman's Cove and often called "Giggle Crack" by the locals (origin unknown). To play it safe, stay well northwest of the point and enter and exit only at Fisherman's Cove if you are taking game.

The sightseer and photgrapher will also do well here. Colorful gorgonia are abundant and make for interesting photo subjects on the wall of the reef. Kelp is present yet very sparse. The garibaldis are everywhere and when it comes to looking for handouts, tame to the point of aggressiveness. Other fish including senoritas, kelpfish, and opaleye are somewhat less friendly but still come within camera range. Look a little harder and you will find octopus, nudibranchs, and an occasional moray.

Conditions at Fisherman's Cove are generally as good as its neighbors—Shaw's and Diver's Coves. In many ways the cove here is actually more protected from southern swells than both Shaw's and Diver's Coves. Diving on the north side of the reef offers some protection from surge of the southerly swell. Visibility here is usually quite good averaging between 15 and 20 feet and reaching to 30 feet quite often. Strong currents are unusual and generally only affect the outer reefs.

If you are familiar with the area, you reach Fisherman's Cove the same way you reach Diver's Cove. Proceed to Laguna Beach via Highway 1 (Coast Highway) and exit toward the beach at Cliff Drive, one block south of the dive shop. Follow Cliff Drive as it turns left. At 631 Cliff Drive is the Laguna Sea Cliff condominums / apartments. The stairs and path leading to Fisherman's Cove is immediately to the right of the apartments' entrance. The top of the path is marked with a blue sign. You may park on the street or at the metered parking in front of Diver's Cove less that 50 feet to the south. There are facilities including showers and restrooms at Heisler Park about 300 feet south of Diver's Cove.

The path that leads to the beach at Fisherman's Cove consists of 37 steps and a gentle incline. The beach is small and sometimes nearly engulfed during extreme high tides. Private residences are very close to the shore so please respect their privacy and be quiet.

Make your entry to the north of the reef. On the south side, between the outer rocks and the point, the reef comes very close to the surface creating hazardous surf. To the north of the reef is sand and a shallow reef with a great deal of eel grass. The bottom drops off quickly over the sand to 10 feet deep within 20 feet of shore.

To the north are shallower reefs that adjoin the south end of Shaw's Cove. Although these reefs are less spectacular, game and a wide variety of marine life are also found here. In the middle of this reef, in about 20 feet of water, is a wide crevice that, at one point, has a crack about 6 inches wide that runs all the way through the reef horizontally. The crack holds two very large morays as well as a potpourri of other sea creatures.

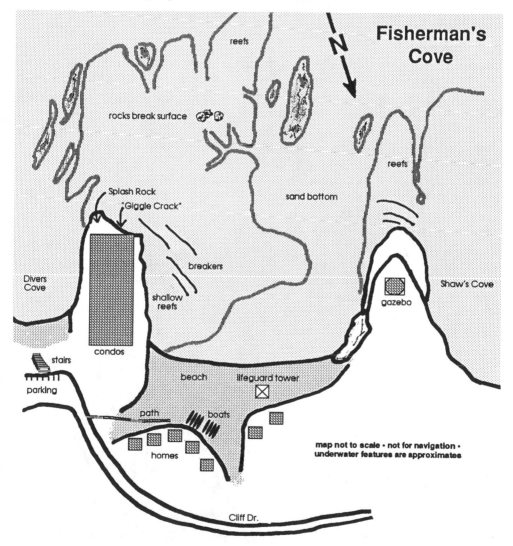

map not to scale · not for navigation · underwater features are approximates

Diver's Cove

Sometimes we just don't feel like climbing mountains. Sometimes ONLY a stroll in the park will do. For those divers who are looking for a dive that just matches the latter description, look toward Laguna Beach and Diver's Cove.

Diver's Cove is a casual yet very rewarding dive with reasonably clear life-filled waters. If you have never made a diving trip to Laguna Beach, start planning; it is worth the trip. Along this small strip of coastline, there are more dive spots than you can shake a snorkel at. Perhaps the easiest of these dive spots is Diver's Cove.

Diver's Cove, surprisingly, does not get its name from the underwater sport but rather from the acrobatic divers that used to use one of the rocks as a diving platform some 40 to 50 years ago. This rocky point, in addition to rocky points to the southeast, protects this cove fairly well under normal conditions. The cove is a sandy beach with reefs extending seaward on the left side of the cove. This reef harbors some of the most abundant and diverse groups of sea life to be found along the Southern California coastline.

In passing over the reefs, one life form seems to dominate the habitat—the bright orange garibaldi fish. Garibaldi at Diver's Cove are so used to divers feeding them that they tend to swarm at the sound of a diver's bubbles. This alone makes Diver's Cove worth visiting. Bring along a stale roll or bagel to promote the feeding frenzy. The playful bright fish will delight you for hours (if your tank lasts that long).

Garibaldi are, of course, not the only fish living on these reefs. Señoritas by the dozens will be right in there feeding with their orange companions. Other fish to look for include the greenish opaleye that like to school in the shallows, bat rays in the sand, and the tiny but bright blue and red gobies hiding in the reef's many crevices.

Invertebrates are abundant as well. In the deeper sections, gold and red gorgonia adorn the rock walls. Nudibranchs like the blue and orange Spanish shawl and yellow sea lemon also can be found. Other fun "touchy-feelies" to be found on these reefs include the shiny chestnut cowry, a variety of colorful anemones, and the large gray moon sponge.

As you may gather, underwater photographers will enjoy this dive spot. Hunters, however, had best go elsewhere. Diver's cove is part of the Heisler Park Ecological Reserve. Nothing is to be taken from or disturbed within the preserve.

To reach Diver's Cove, get on Coast Highway (Highway 1) and head for Laguna Beach. Divers Cove is a half mile northwest of Laguna's main beach. Turn toward the sea at Hawthorne Road and when you reach Cliff Drive you will be facing Diver's Cove. There are a small number of metered parking spaces right on the small bluff overlooking the cove. If the metered parking is full or you are out of quarters, there is also parking along Cliff Drive.

After parking, the walk to the small sandy beach is easy down a few steps and short ramp. On the beach is a lifeguard tower and, if present, the lifeguard will make sure you are diving with a buddy (as you should be) and that you are familiar with local conditions. With good conditions, entry is usually easy. A slight swell, however, sometimes creates short plunging breakers that can take you by surprise during water entry and exits.

Most of the reef that is of interest to divers will be to the right side of the cove. On the point, shallow finger reefs covered in eel grass extend seaward. Lying in 15 feet of water or less, these reefs are excellent for snorkeling when conditions are calm. Further out and to the right around the point are the

deeper reefs that scuba divers are most interested in. Some of these reefs can be quite large rising as much as 10 feet from a sand bottom. Large cracks and crevices in some of these rocks make very interesting exploring. Depths average 25 to 35 feet. Visibility is usually good averaging 15 to 20 feet, and frequently reaching 40 feet in calm winter conditions.

Diver's Cove is, however, but one small diving area of the many diving opportunities of Laguna Beach. Just to the south is Picnic Beach and its offshore reefs covered in kelp. To the north, just around the point, is Fisherman's Cove (Boat Canyon). Many divers, as a matter of fact, make a loop trip on their dive by entering at Diver's Cove and exiting at Fisherman's Cove (or visa versa). You may wish to spend the day diving this section of the coast. There are several dive stores in the area to provide air fills or gear rentals. There are also many eateries nearby varying from hamburger stands to posh restaurants. Just up the road a few steps from Diver's Cove is Heisler Park where you will find showers, restrooms, and a pleasant picnic area.

Climbing mountains can be spectacular and rewarding. But when all you need is a walk in the park, try Diver's Cove for a pleasant low-key dive.

Picnic Beach

If there is any one place along the Laguna Beach coastline where shore diving can be done at a leisurely pace, it is at Picnic Beach. On the bluff overlooking the kelp-filled waters is a beautiful park with restrooms, picnic benches, and barbecues. The beach is wide, calm, and generally uncrowded.

Almost immediately offshore from this beautiful beach are a series of reefs that extend to over 100 yards offshore into depths of 40 feet or more. The reefs are made up of parallel ridges rising as much as 10 feet off the clean, sandy bottom. In the reef are large cracks, crevices, and overhangs. In one particular spot, a narrow tunnel passes entirely underneath a 20-foot wide reef (too narrow for passage by divers). All of this combines to create a rich environment for marine life.

Garibaldis are, of course, everywhere. They make their presence known immediately and are always looking for a handout. Other bountiful and colorful varieties of fish on these reefs include senoritas, opaleye, and bluebanded gobies. Attached to the rocks are colorful anemones, giant keyhole limpets, gorgonia, large gray-colored moon sponges and the flashy Spanish shawl nudibranchs.

The photographer and sightseer will not only enjoy the creatures but also the usually good visibility this dive spot offers. 15 to 20 feet of visibility is common and it has been known to reach up to 40 feet in the winter.

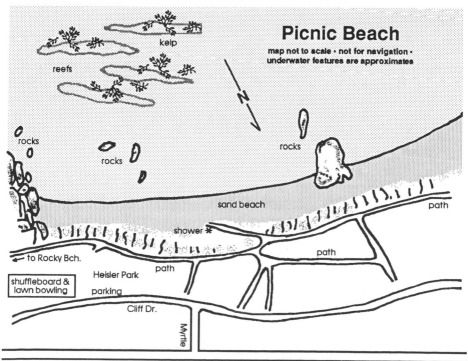

Picnic Beach

map not to scale · not for navigation ·
underwater features are approximates

kelp

reefs

N

rocks

rocks

rocks

sand beach

path

shower

path

path

← to Rocky Bch.

path

shuffleboard &
lawn bowling

Heisler Park
parking

Cliff Dr.

Myrtle

Coast Hwy. (Hwy. 1)

Kelp also attaches itself to the reef. The strands are tall and healthy although not thick. Passage through the kelp is easy and observations of the sea life that accumulates at its bases and in the fronds is very rewarding.

The entire area is a marine preserve. Hunting is not welcome and sightseers should take nothing but pictures.

For those of you already familiar with diving this area, reaching Picnic Cove is quite simple. Picnic Cove is directly south, down the coast, from popular Diver's Cove. Turn toward the sea off Coast Highway (Highway 1) onto Myrtle. Myrtle will end at Cliff Drive. Metered parking is available to the right and left along Cliff Drive. Crowds in the summer can be a problem and early

arrival is a must. The ramp to the beach is slightly to the right and through the park. The park has excellent picnic facilities (hence the beach's name) and restrooms are located a few steps north of the top of the path to the beach. At the foot of the path is a single freshwater shower (not always operable).

The cove is somewhat protected so entry is usually easy. Avoid the center of the beach as there are rocks in the surf that break surface at low tide.

The close-in reefs are marked by sparse kelp and lie in 25 to 35 feet of water. The thicker kelp to the south is more easily reached by entering at Rocky Beach directly down the coast.

Rocky Beach

Shaw's, Fisherman's, and Diver's Coves, along with Picnic Beach, are great spots for diving in Laguna Beach, but if you want to avoid the underwater crowds, try Rocky Beach. Diving here is a little more challenging but you may find it extra rewarding as well.

Overlooking the diving area from the small bluff makes it apparent why this is a good dive location. There is a huge kelp bed extending from 50 to 200 yards offshore. The shoreline is varied, offering a number of possible entry/

exit points. Approximately 100 yards offshore is a large reef breaking the surface at mid-to-low tide which in turn is surrounded by numerous smaller reefs; this results in a huge diving area large enough to accommodate many divers in an uncrowded way.

Perhaps another reason fewer divers visit here is that the entry appears more difficult. Neighboring Diver's Cove, Picnic Beach, and Main Beach all have easy sand-beach entry whereas Rocky Beach is just as its name states—rocky. A diver choosing to dive here should have some rock-surf entry experience. There are, however, several good easy entry points from which to choose making them fairly simple in small or moderate surf.

Close to shore, the bottom drops off quickly to 10 to 15 feet. There are many small, low-lying reefs covered heavily with eel grass and interspersed with sand patches and channels. The

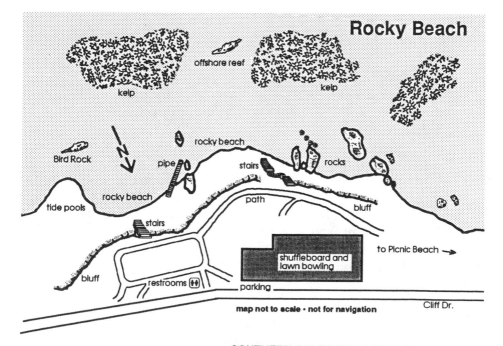

shallow reefs are excellent for snorkeling with little surf, but scuba here can be difficult in moderate surf because of surge.

If on scuba, there is no reason to linger in the shallows because deeper water lies only a few more fin strokes toward the sea. The larger reefs, particularly the one that breaks the surface at low tide, can be quite spectacular. The rock walls of the reefs drop quickly and often vertically in 20 to 30 feet of water and then slope to 40 or 50 feet. Much of the surrounding area has the growth of healthy kelp.

Critters that call these rocks home include crabs of several varieties, large and colorful anemones and broad stands of gorgonia. Photographers will be delighted with the cooperative garibaldis and senortia fish as well as being surprised by more unusual visitors such as horn sharks and yellowtail.

There is other game in the area including lobster, halibut, scallops and game fish. Look only! The entire area is a marine preserve and taking anything in the marine environment is prohibited. The marine preseve provides an excellent opportunity to observe creatures in the wild not always found elsewhere along the coast.

Reaching Rocky Beach is particularly simple if you are familiar with the popular diving area. It lies just south of Diver's Cove and Picnic Beach. Coast Highway (Highway 1) passes directly through the town of Laguna Beach. Turn on Jasmine St. just north of the center of town. The stairs to the water's edge are just behind the shuffleboard and lawn bowling courts. There are two sets of stairs providing a number of water entry/exit possiblities. There is metered parking along Cliff Drive. Try to arrive early during summer weekends as parking is limited. Bring lots of quarters— buying time on the meter can add up quickly

The beautiful park through which you pass to reach the beach is Heisler Park. This park has excellent facilities including showers, restrooms, and picnic sites. The walkway along the bluff provides views of the diving area from a number of different angles. Study your dive plan carefully from here for a flawless dive.

Main Beach

Laguna Beach in South Orange County has long been noted for its excellent diving with access to water's edge easily reached. In addition, the waters are generally clear and remarkably full of life. The most popular beach with tourists and sun seekers is Main Beach directly off the center of town. In the summer, and at other times of the year as well, this beach is often quite crowded. For this reason, many divers avoid this dive spot for other less crowded spots nearby. What many divers are unaware of is the superb kelp beds and reefs that lie less than 150 yards from shore on the north end of the beach.

Marked by a large rounded rock known as Bird Rock, the reef begins in as shallow as 10 feet of water . Bird Rock is only 50 to 100 feet from shore, depending on the tide; and just beyond the rock, is a huge expanse of kelp that extends over 200 yards offshore, for nearly 1/2 mile to the north. The reef under the kelp canopy is nearly as extensive. Ranging in depths from 20 to nearly 50 feet, the reef is full of crevices, boulders and ledges. All of this creates an excellent environment for a bonanza of marine life.

All of Laguna Beach's dive spots are famous for abundant and friendly bright orange garibaldi. The reefs off Main Beach are no exception. If you have never spent an entire dive feeding, observing, and playing with these

wonderful fish, you are missing a relaxing and delightful experience. If you can pull yourself away from the garibaldi, take time to look around at the colorful collection of invertebrates. Although not as abundant as in other Laguna Beach locations, there is enough variety to keep macro photographers busy.

Hunters will be tempted by resident populations of abalone, lobster and game fish. Abalone taking is strictly forbidden as the entire area falls into the abalone moratorium zone. Taking of other game is questionable. The reef in question is cut in half by the borders of the Heisler Park Ecological Preserve in which no marine life is to be taken. Because it's difficult to pick out man-made imaginary borders on the sea floor, it is recommended that you take nothing from this area. If you are interested in game, there are plenty of reefs with more bountiful game to the south.

Access to Main Beach is quite good. Sunbathers use the access directly in front of the lifeguard tower. Although this eliminates a short stair climb, the best entry point for diving is a moderately long walk to the north and parking is very limited. A better access point would be from the small bluffs at Heisler Park.

Turn toward the beach on Cliff Drive and within a block, just beside the Las Brisas Mexican Restaurant, is the access to the shore. Here, at the extreme south end of Heisler Park, is a large gazebo on the point overlooking the diving area. This is an excellent vantage point to study the lay of the kelp, reef patterns, prevailing conditions, and shore entry and exit points. Metered parking is available along Cliff Drive so bring lots of quarters. The path to the beach is just to the left of the gazebo. Entry can be made in a number of points but most divers prefer to enter off the sand beach. There are numerous shallow rocks and reefs in the surf zone but the bottom generally drops off quickly to 10 feet deep.

Should you find the diving good enough for a second tank of air, there are several dive stores within a mile of the dive site. There are also many other excellent dive sites to the north and south. Within a few blocks to the north are the famous dive sites of Rocky and Picnic Beach and Diver's, Fisherman's, and Shaw's Cove. Between dives, Laguna Beach is an excellent place to pass some time. As previously mentioned, there is a Mexican restaurant on the bluff above the dive site. Although this restaurant is a little on the expensive side, there are a number of other eateries in the area with a wide variety of price ranges. If you are feeling cultural, check out the famous Laguna Beach Museum of Art just inland of the Mexican restaurant.

Cress Street

Experienced lobster hunters know that when the tasty crustaceans cannot be found in their usual habitat of crevices and caves, a likely place to look is in shallow spots among the eel grass (*Zostera marina*). Eel grass is the long stringy green plant that grows in thick bunches and patches in shallow rocky reef areas and lobsters often love to hide in it.

Eel grass is particularly prolific in the surf and surge zones along the popular Southern California beach diving areas of Laguna Beach. Laguna Beach is so popular with divers, however, that lobster have become scarce in the more heavily frequented areas. One of the dive sites that still contains a fair amount of lobster among the eel grass, not to mention a beautiful reef farther out, is off the beach at Cress Street.

The bottom off the sandy beach drops quickly to 10 or 15 feet deep over a bed of strewn rocks and ridge reefs. Looking out from shore, it is easy to spot the inner and outer reefs breaking the surface in the surge. The inner reef is a short swim of 45 to 60 yards and the outer reef is about 100 to 150 yards out. There is a great deal of rocks, ridges and kelp in between. On the inside, eel grass and feather boa kelp are the predominate plant species. This is the surgy shallow area where lobster like to hide under the swaying green mop.

Farther out, the reefs on the bottom begin to take on a more regular pattern of being parallel to shore and 30 feet or so apart. They are fairly low to the bottom, rising only five feet or so but an occasional rocky spire juts up as much as 10 feet. Some of these rock formations take on rather peculiar shapes. Giant kelp growth begins in about 20 feet of water and the waters surrounding the lush growth teem with life. This is a good area for hunting kelp bass. They are very leery of divers but a skilled spearfisherman should be able to get within range.

If you are not the hunter type, this is where the scenery begins to blossom. Garibaldis are abundant and friendly. If you are carrying a camera, try photographing their stark orange color against the rich green of the eel grass. Wide angle photography is usually best as the frequent surge makes close-ups difficult.

Moving further out, large stretches of sand break up the bottom until you reach the outer reef. It is over this sand that spearfisherman may get lucky and see a halibut. Photographers and sightseers should stick near the edges of the kelp forest and look for bat rays and angel sharks. There is also an abundance of señorita fish, kelpfish, and opaleye. Seals have also been known to frolic over these reefs.

The outer reef is a large house-size boulder rising from the bottom 25 feet below to just break the surface. Surrounding this monolith are smaller auto-sized boulders probably broken off from the mother rock. In the crevices one can find moray eels, rock fish, octopus, and, if you're lucky, an occasional lobster. Growing over the rocks are a large variety of algae, a few scallops, and colorful anemones. Eyes should also be kept open for the brightly colored lemon and Spanish shawl nudibranchs and tiny bluebanded gobies.

Surge is a little less prevalent out here but still can be a problem. Just for the thrill of it, take a ride through the surge across the top of the rock. If you can stand the excitement, the power of the ocean will toss you about and exhilarate you. Surrounding the rock is a lush kelp forest with countless more environs to explore. For the really strong swimmers, the reef continues out into deeper water and become even more exciting.

Crowds do not frequent Cress Street for one very simple reason: water entry conditions are not usually ideal. The beach is exposed and the beach slope is sharp which leads to a short but powerful surf zone. Experience in surf entries is a must. Dive this spot only on days of two feet or less of surf. To dive it in any greater surf is not necessarily dangerous but frustrating. If you make it out past the pounding surf the bottom will then to be very surgy. The good news is Laguna Beach has generally low surf conditions 50 to 60 percent of the year.

More good news is that if Cress Street is not divable, there are plenty of better protected spots like Shaw's or Diver's Cove only a few miles away. Visibility here is variable. If the rest of Laguna Beach is clear, and the surf is down, it will be good here as well. Surf three feet or larger creates a strong surge lifting the sediment off the bottom.

Access to this dive site is reached by turning on to Cress Street off Pacific Coast Highway to the south of the center of town. Parking is limited to just a handful of metered spaces. A little less than 70 steps lead to the pleasant sandy beach below. Pause at the top of the steps for a good observation of the near-shore reefs below. You will be able to see where the various reefs break the surface, the borders of the kelp forest, and how the shore break is laying out. There is a lifeguard tower on the beach that is manned during the summer. Other than that, there are no facilities.

But not to worry: the small beach is right at the town's doorstep. In Laguna Beach there are a number of fine restaurants as well as the usual fast food joints. Bring your non-diving loved ones as they can spend the day exploring Laguna's fine shopping districts and art galleries. There are also several dive stores in Laguna Beach to satisfy your scuba needs and answer questions.

Woods Cove

It is not unusual to see several hundred divers assaulting the beaches in southern Orange County on any given weekend during the summer; however, not to worry about the crowds. Laguna Beach offers enough quantity and variety of dive spots where one can obtain true submarine solitude. One of the lesser-known dive locations in Laguna Beach is Woods Cove. Woods Cove offers all the qualities you would expect to find in a Laguna Beach dive spot without some of the crowds.

First, marine life is both abundant and colorful. Garibaldis that feed from your hand are plentiful on the reef which is on the east side of the cove. On the rocks, a colorful array of invertebrates can be found including nudibranchs, a variety of anenomes, gorgonia, and starfish. On the western reef is a small kelp forest.

Woods Cove is not part of a marine reserve; hence, the taking of game is legal under normal California Fish and Game regulations. Lobster can be found but is sparse; try in shallow depths where they are often overlooked. Scallops are also present in small numbers. Abalone are illegal to take here as this cove falls into the moritorium area. Some species of game fish including kelp bass and sheepshead are present on the outer edges of the reefs. Halibut can sometimes be found on the sand between the reefs.

Perhaps the most interesting feature of this dive spot is its bottom terrain. Two main reefs dominate the bottom of the cove. To the east, starting approximately 50 yards out is a reef made up of large jumbled boulders and rock outcroppings. The rocks lie in such a way as to create large crevices, overhangs and caves. The sand bottom averages 30 to 40 feet deep about 100 yards out but the reef reaches to the surface as much as 15 feet in spots. To the west is a relatively low-lying kelp-covered reef with this interesting sidelight: In the middle of the western reef is a huge boulder that rises from the 30-foot-deep bottom to within a few feet of the surface. The resultant walls and overhangs the boulder creates makes for interesting explo-

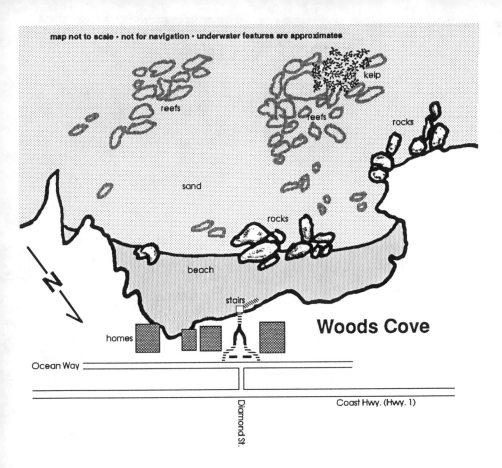

ration.

Access to the cove is quite easy. The cove is located in the southern portion of the town of Laguna Beach (not South Laguna) about two miles down the coast from the popular dive spots of Diver's and Shaw's Cove. Exit Coast Highway (Hwy. 1) on Diamond Street. Diamond will intersect and end at Ocean Way. It is here that stairs lead to the beach and cove. Parking is limited but free along Diamond Street and Ocean Way. The stairs lead through a pleasant garden between private residences, so please be considerate.

The sand beach on the cove is divided in the middle by a large boulder formation. Entry is usually done best to the left of the boulder on the east side of the cove. Beware of submerged rocks that break the surface at low tide. Surf entry during the winter is usually easy in calm conditions but during the summer, a southerly swell can make diving difficult.

Moss Street

Another Laguna Beach dive spot that is perhaps less frequented by the crowds is the small cove located at the end of Moss Street. The reefs of Moss Street hold diving pleasures that are as good as any other location in Laguna Beach. There are small walls and ledges and, in spots, the rocks tower as high as 18 feet from the sand bottom. Here and there are deep cracks and crevices that cut into the reef and resemble caves.

The rocks are also thickly covered by a wide variety of marine life. From about 50 yards out to the seaward ends of the reefs, gorgonia are plentiful. In spots, the rocks seem overgrown with golden-colored gorgonian growth. Feather worms and colorful anemones also make for good subjects for underwater photographers and in the surrounding waters, friendly garibaldi are at every turn of the fin.

The hunter may also fare well here. Although sparse and on the small side, lobster can be taken here when in season; an occasional small scallop can be pried from the rocks and the spearfisherman will find sheepshead and kelp bass. The outer reefs are best for the bigger game. A large halibut or two sometimes hides in the sand between the reefs.

Conditions at the Moss Street cove are generally good year round. The cove is well protected and currents rarely affect the area except on the extreme outer

reef. Visibility is good, as in most Laguna Beach dive spots. Averaging between 15 and 25 feet, the visibility can reach as much as 35 feet and is seldom below 10 feet. The shallow parts of the reef can have a surge problem but this can easily be avoided by moving to the deeper (30 to 35 feet) sections of the reef about 100 to 150 yards offshore.

The path that leads to this picturesque cove is easily found by exiting Coast Highway (Highway 1) onto Moss Street a little over one mile south of downtown. After about a block, Moss Street will dead-end. Limited parking is available on Moss Street and nearby Ocean Way. Parking is sometimes filled in which case it is a simple matter to drop your gear at the top of the stairs and park a few blocks away. Be aware of "no parking" red zones; they are everywhere. Also, the entire area is residential—please respect their quiet and privacy.

There are 62 steps leading to the small sandy beach from the end of Moss Street. From the landing at the top of the stairs, ocean conditions can be carefully observed. A gentle rip is common in the middle of the cove. Note

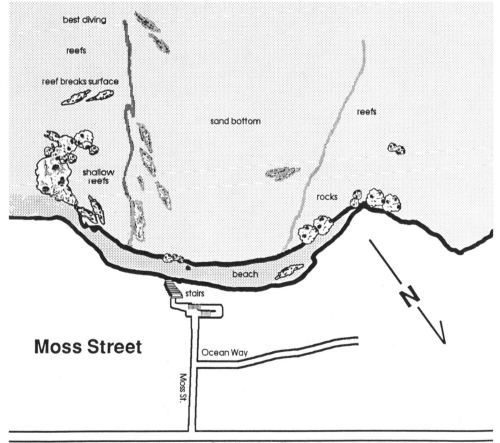

best diving

reefs

reef breaks surface

sand bottom

reefs

shallow reefs

rocks

beach

stairs

Moss Street

Ocean Way

Moss St.

Coast Hwy. (Hwy. 1)

map not to scale · not for navigation · underwater features are approximates

the rocks that break the surface in the swell at low tide off the point to the south and closer in on the northwest side of the cove. The rocks of the southerly point, known as Moss Point, marks the beginning of the reef that is of most interest to divers. There are reefs on the northwest side on the cove but they tend to be low- lying and sparse on sea life. Farther to the northwest lies Woods Cove which is another dive spot worth exploring.

Upon entering, the bottom drops off rapidly five or six feet. Beware of loose stones in the surf as they are common and can hinder entry and exit. This shallow water close to the beach is good for snorkelers on very calm days.

Once again, the best reef is to the south, so stay to your left as you face the ocean. If you drop to the bottom, just beyond the rocks breaking the surface, you will avoid the majority of the surge. Beyond these rocks the reef breaks up into a jumble of large boulders that create overhangs, crevices and small caves to explore.

Farther out, the rocks taper off and patch reefs can be found across the sand. On the other side of this reef, to the south a few yards, the rocks ascend vertically in spots creating large overhangs; it is here the reef is split in spots forming large crevices. After exiting the water, relaxing on the sand in the secluded cove at Moss Street may be just the thing after a fine day of diving.

1,000 Steps

One of the most spectacular dive sights off of the Laguna Beach area is largely ignored simply because it takes a bit of effort to reach it. The name of the dive site—1,000 Steps—explains it all. While there are actually "only" 220 steps, all of them are steep and magnified by the weight of scuba gear. And while it may be a tough, long haul after the dive, what lies in the waters just beyond the steps may make the effort very worthwhile.

For starters, there is a spectacular underwater arch in 15 feet of water less than 100 yards from shore. At 20 feet wide and about eight feet high at the peak, the arch is large enough for several divers to fit in. The surge whips in the shallow arch making great fun for the diver who wants to play "thread the needle" in the arch.

The second reason for braving the steep stairs is as compelling as the first: lobster. While certainly not overflowing with the tasty crustacean, this is perhaps one of the most heavily populated locations off Laguna Beach with adequate shore access.

The lobsters make their homes in a maze of boulders and reefs that are fascinating to explore. Depths range from a surgy five feet to a small kelp bed on the outside that has a sand bottom nearby at 30 feet down.

But it is up among the shallow reefs where the diver is likely to have the most

fun. In depths ranging from 15 to 25 feet, there are large crevices, 5 to 10 feet wide, that beg to be explored. At the bottom of the crevices are jumbles of boulders and large rock overhangs where lobster and other creatures love to hide. Look closely and you will find moray eels, kelp bass and an occasional rock scallop.

On the rock faces are nudibranchs, starfish, and the tiny, brightly colored, bluebanded goby fish. Darting in and out of the crevices are numerous friendly garibaldi. Also present are large schools of opaleye and surfperch. The tops of the reefs are blanketed with eel and surf grass as well as feather boa kelp. Also look under this green blanket, as an occasional lobster can be found hiding there.

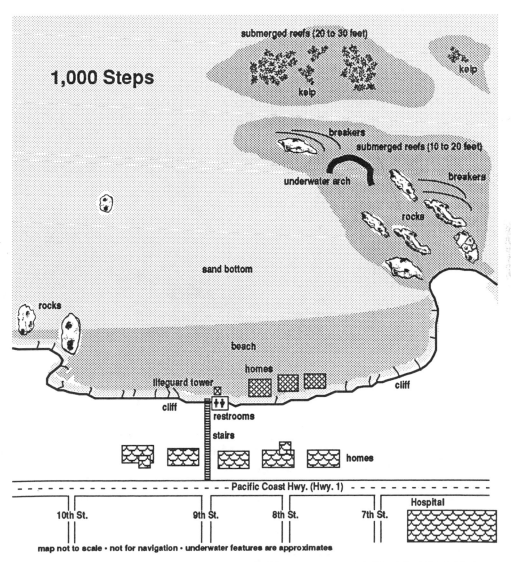

1,000 Steps

submerged reefs (20 to 30 feet)

kelp

kelp

breakers

submerged reefs (10 to 20 feet)

underwater arch

breakers

rocks

sand bottom

rocks

beach

homes

lifeguard tower

cliff

cliff

restrooms

stairs

homes

- - Pacific Coast Hwy. (Hwy. 1) - - - - - - - - -

10th St.   9th St.   8th St.   7th St.

Hospital

map not to scale · not for navigation · underwater features are approximates

If surf conditions are low, diving conditions are usually as good here as anywhere else along Laguna. This is an unprotected beach, however, and anytime the surf is three feet or higher, divers should seek alternate dive sights. The beach slope is steep with water depths dropping to 10 to 15 feet only a few yards from shore. This can create a "plunging" wave that can drop a diver quickly.

Surge is generally strong here, but this can be both a problem and an asset. A mild surge in the large crevices can make for a lot of fun—a roller coaster ride if you will. The diver experienced with surge can use it to shoot in, out and over reefs. If surge riding is not your cup of tea, try the outer kelp bed where the effects of the surge are much weaker.

Visibility is generally good if the surf is down. Over the reefs, it averages 10 to 20 feet with occasional days of 30 feet or more.

To reach the beach access point at the top of the stairs, take Pacific Coast Highway to the town of South Laguna Beach. The access is across Pacific Coast Highway from 9th Street. Parking is limited to the opposite side of the highway and the side streets. Perhaps the most hazardous part of this dive trip is trying to cross busy Pacific Coast Highway! At the top of the stairs take the time to read the signs. They point out that this is a marine preserve and that taking of anything other than what is listed on the sign is prohibited (it is okay to take lobster and most game fish, but not scallops or abalone). A second sign points out that the beach closes at 9:00 p.m., so schedule any night dives carefully.

About two-thirds of the way down the steps you will be able to view the dive area off the point to the right. Broken rocks extend from the point. Several rocks break the surface in the swell. It is between two of these rocks that you will find the underwater arch.

At the bottom of the steps is a lifeguard tower, showers, and restrooms. Water entry is best from the right end of the broad sandy beach, directly in front of the reefs.

If you are into roller coaster rides, this may be just the dive for you.

Introduction to San Diego County

Diving the coastline of San Diego can be very rewarding if you are either very experienced at diving the area, or know specifically where to go for easy, relaxing diving. Much of the shore diving off this county can be very difficult, particularly in the northern sections. Large surf, difficult entries and murky water are the norm along the north San Diego County coastline.

This area is not without its fine reefs and good shore access however. Reefs with healthy kelp beds are located in several locations anywhere from 200 yards to 1/4-mile offshore which means long swims to reach the best diving. Some of these locations include (from north to south) San Onofre, Oceanside Pier, and Carlsbad State Beach. Moonlight State Beach is good for game. Farther south, Sea Cliff Park (also known by locals as "Swamis") is perhaps the best location in the north San Diego County. Surf here can still be quite large, but kelp, good diving, and clear water is fairly close to shore.

San Elijo State Park is an excellent beach campground but diving is a long

swim away through usually large surf. Other access points farther south include Tide County Park, and 13th and 8th Streets in Del Mar.

Just south of Del Mar is the northern border of the San Diego-La Jolla Underwater Park. The park includes many popular dive sites southward to La Jolla Cove but is a marine preserve where no invertebrates can be taken except abalone, clams, crab, lobster, and sea urchin. Within this park is the San Diego-La Jolla Ecological Reserve which includes such popular dive sites as La Jolla Canyon, Goldfish Point and La Jolla Cove. Nothing—animal, plant or otherwise—may be taken or disturbed.

La Jolla Canyon is a submarine canyon with two branches. The northern branch, known as Scripps

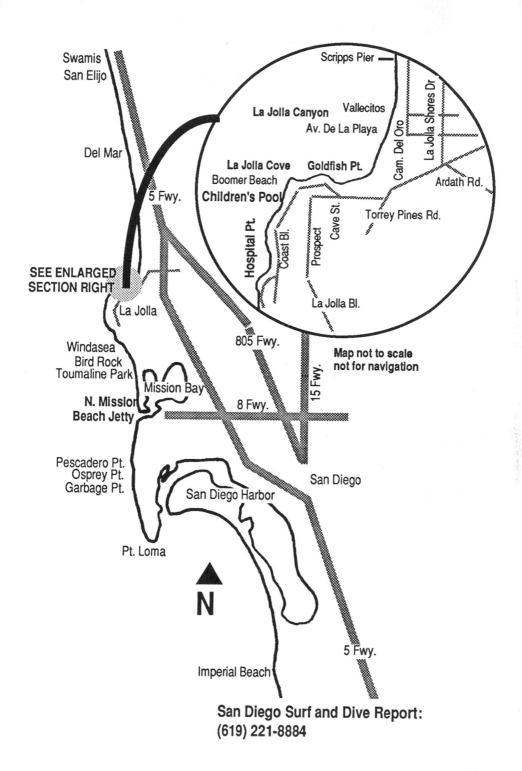

Swamis
San Elijo

Del Mar

5 Fwy.

Scripps Pier

La Jolla Canyon
Av. De La Playa

Vallecitos

La Jolla Shores Dr

Cam. Del Oro

La Jolla Cove
Boomer Beach
Children's Pool

Goldfish Pt.

Ardath Rd.

Torrey Pines Rd.

Hospital Pt.

Coast Bl.

Prospect

Cave St.

La Jolla Bl.

SEE ENLARGED
SECTION RIGHT

La Jolla

805 Fwy.

Map not to scale
not for navigation

Windasea
Bird Rock
Toumaline Park

Mission Bay

15 Fwy.

N. Mission
Beach Jetty

8 Fwy.

Pescadero Pt.
Osprey Pt.
Garbage Pt.

San Diego

San Diego Harbor

Pt. Loma

N

5 Fwy.

Imperial Beach

San Diego Surf and Dive Report:
(619) 221-8884

Canyon, is the most spectacular with diving best done from a boat by experienced divers as many of the canyon walls are vertical. The southern branch of the canyon comes to within 100 to 150 yards of shore near the popular La Jolla Shores Beach. Although not as spectacular as the Scripps Canyon, the La Jolla Branch has several vertical drops of 20 to 30 feet. The water is usually clear and offers one of the most unusual beach dives along the coast of Southern California.

The coast then turns from sandy beach to rocky cliffs along the La Jolla Bay. Access to the rocky shore can be found at Goldfish Point; diving the La Jolla Caves and the point are easy from here. La Jolla Cove is the most popular beach location in San Diego County. Crowds can be a problem but diving is usually good in clean, life-filled waters.

Around the corner from La Jolla Cove, the beach faces west and is much more open to the effects of the sea. There are access points at Boomer Beach and Shell Beach but heavy surf and unpredictable rips and currents are a constant problem. Children's Pool (Casa Pool) is a small cove created by an artificial breakwater. Calm water entries and exits are possible into clear water. Hospital Point is open to the weather, but under the right conditions can offer very good diving between rocky ledges.

Farther south there are access points along the Windansea Beach area. Little Point and Big Rock are diving spots along this beach that can be difficult to dive because of high surf and dirty water. North and South Bird Rock are good locations for abalone in shallow water but little else. South of the Bird Rock, there is good beach access at Sun Gold Point and Tourmaline Park but swims are long through murky water and high surf. On the far end of Mission Beach, fairly decent diving can sometimes be found on the north Mission Beach Jetty.

South of the Mission Bay Channel, there are several points that provide beach access but often difficult entries into murky waters. Some of these locations are Pescadero, Osprey, and Lascombs Points. Hunting at these locations can sometimes be good but scenery is poor. Visibility improves slightly off spots known as Rock Slide, Rock Pile and Garbage Points. Diving in the Point Loma kelp beds is excellent but there is no shore access and a boat is required.

Imperial Beach and Tijuana Sloughs are in the southern portion of the county. There is an old submarine shipwreck off Imperial Beach if you know where to look. Lobster and halibut can also be found at the Sloughs even though water visibility in these areas is very poor.

La Jolla Submarine Canyon

"The training ground for the San Diego diver" is what one diver dubbed it after stepping from the surf at La Jolla Shores. He had just finished a satisfying dive into the La Jolla Canyon. A class of twelve neophyte divers was entering the water as he and his buddy exited. Another pair of experienced divers bobbed in the swells just offshore.

What makes La Jolla Canyon a continual favorite of San Diego divers of all skill levels? Some reasons include good facilities, easy surf entry, and excellent shore access. But the prevailing reason is simply great diving. Offshore, 100 to 150 yards out, in 35 to 70 feet of water, the ocean floor drops away in nearly vertical walls to depths of over 800 feet. The walls and terraces of the La Jolla canyon provide some of the most unusual and spectacular beach diving that Southern California has to offer.

Access to the submarine canyon is off the popular beach of La Jolla Shores just north of La Jolla Bay. The beach has excellent facilities and ample parking.

Generally, the best point at which to enter the water is directly off a small steel and concrete lifeguard tower marked #20. This tower is immediately south of the main lifeguard tower in front of the park and just north of Vallecitos Street. The main tower is manned year round and posts diving

conditions daily. The lifeguards also have at their disposal a rescue boat stationed on the beach. To the north of the main tower is the surfing area; diving here is discouraged. South of Vallecitos Street, at the end of Avenida De La Playa, is a small boat launching area; stay clear of this area also.

Out from tower #20, the sand bottom slopes moderately. Head directly out from the tower about 100 yards; then, line yourself up so that the end of Scripp's pier (to the north) is directly under the green building on the ridge in the distance. This will place you just inshore from the rim of the canyon in about 40 feet of water.

The canyon here drops from 50 feet in a series of ledges that vary in height from 10 to 20 feet. The bottom drops off rapidly to over 200 feet. The sensation of looking into the depths from the rim of the canyon can be exhilarating. Visibility averages around 15 to 20 feet but can drop severely with heavy surf or plankton blooms. 30-to-40-foot visibility occurs when upwelling from the canyon is present.

The upwelling can also bring deep water species near the rim for observation. One of these visitors is squid in the late fall and early spring. Other large fish are then in turn attracted by the squid for feeding.

On the clay canyon walls, several varieties of small colorful fish make their home. Small branches of gorgonia are attached to the ledges below 65 feet with crab and octopus making their homes in the holes in the clay walls.

Look but don't touch! This entire area is an underwater park and ecological reserve. Nothing is to be taken or disturbed.

After your dive, you can make use of the outdoor freshwater showers located on the restroom building just behind tower #20. To top off your day, you can bring a picnic lunch to enjoy leisurely in the park. The park also makes an excellent staging area for an organized group dive.

Goldfish Point

Just north of central San Diego lies the beautiful community of La Jolla. The community sits on an extension into the Pacific Ocean where diving opportunities abound. The north coast of La Jolla forms La Jolla Bay which, as a north-facing bay, is naturally protected, making this an excellent calm-water area during times of southerly swells. The southern section of the bay is surrounded by sandstone cliffs. Cut into these cliffs is the famous La Jolla Cove and La Jolla Caves, and between them, the small peninsula know as Goldfish Point.

The point is appropriately named for the garibaldi that often congregate there. They are very used to the divers and so are always looking for a free lunch. They often surrround any diver that may have a handout.

Goldfish Point lies within the La Jolla Underwater Park which prohibits the taking or disturbing of any marine life. As a consequence, lobster, octopus and other normally shy creatures can be observed undisturbed. Invertebrates such as starfish and anemones are also present and create a good backdrop for photographers.

The variable bottom creates interesting diving and photography as well. Reefs covered by eel grass drop to a sand bottom only 50 yards out while other ledges and sand channels also make for interesting exploration.

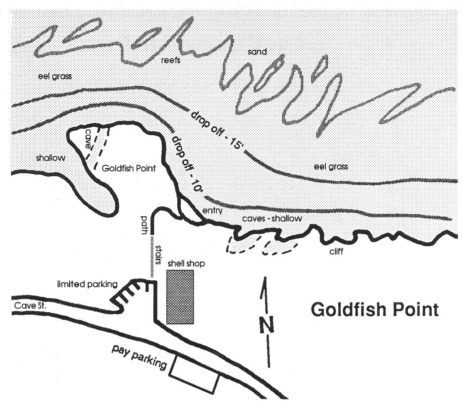

reefs

sand

eel grass

drop off - 15'

drop off - 10'

cave

shallow

Goldfish Point

eel grass

entry

caves - shallow

path

stairs

shell shop

cliff

limited parking

Cave St.

N

Goldfish Point

pay parking

map not to scale · not for navigation · underwater features are approximates

   Access to the diving area adjacent to the point can be made in either of two ways. The most direct is via a path down the point located behind the La Jolla Cave Curio Shop. The stairs and short, steep path lead to a small rock shelf at water's edge that is perfect for entries but only in the calmest weather. The second choice is to enter at La Jolla Cove and swim to the point some 200 yards away.

   Goldfish Point is a good alternative during crowded days if you have your heart set on diving the La Jolla area. Across from the Curio Shop is an underground parking area that affords easy access from your car to the top of the path. The cost is not cheap, but it beats driving around for hours looking for a place to park.

La Jolla Cove

Second only to the La Jolla Canyon, La Jolla Cove is perhaps the most popular dive site in San Diego. It is also an extremely popular spot for local beach lovers. As a consequence, if you want to dive La Jolla Cove on the summer weekends, be prepared to battle with the crowds but don't let them stop you from diving this excellent spot.

La Jolla Cove lies on the northernmost extension of the La Jolla Peninsula. The cove faces north, protecting it from the predominately southerly swell that batters the area during the summer. As a result, the cove is a good dive for the summer months.

Out from the small sandy cove are a variety of rocky ledges, reefs and sand channels. Around the point to the northwest, known by locals as "Alligator Head," the sea life becomes quite abundant. Friendly garibaldi are, of course, everywhere. If you are lucky, you may spot a broomtail grouper that is making a slow comeback to the area. Seals are also frequent visitors and are quite used to the divers. On the bottom and in the reefs you will find moray eels, lobster and rockfish that are surprisingly friendly. Their lack of fear is understandable; the diving area lies within the San Diego- La Jolla Underwater Ecological Reserve. Nothing is to be taken or disturbed.

On the other side of the cove, similar conditions exist. The rocky ledges are

fairly close to shore all the way to Goldfish Point. Depths on the reefs are a maximum of 30 feet. Farther out, in deeper water, the bottom turns to sand. Angel sharks and halibut can sometimes be observed out here but little else.

Perhaps the biggest challenge in diving La Jolla Cove is finding a place to park. You will have your best luck early in the mornings or on weekdays or both. Parking ajacent to the Ellen Browning Scripps Memorial Park (which overlooks the cove) is very limited. There are no parking meters but there is a three-hour time limit. The park overlooking the cove has all the facilities you should need: restrooms, showers, telephones, picnic areas, and large grassy areas for suiting up.

There is a lifeguard stand that overlooks the cove. Posted on the stand is daily water and surf conditions. If you are unfamiliar with the area, a quick check with the lifeguard will be helpful. It is always a good idea to call the surf-and-water report before your trip. Although the cove is somewhat protected, large surf and surge are not uncommon.

It is only a few stairs down to the small sandy beach in the middle of the cove; water entry is best here.

A few spots to avoid are "the hole," an indentation in the cliffs on the east side of the cove that seems to generate rips and unpredictable currents, and a dangerous shallow reef farther to the east.

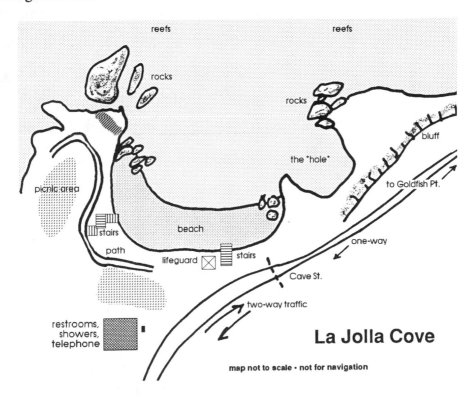

La Jolla Cove

map not to scale · not for navigation

Children's Pool
(a.k.a. Casa Pool)

   South of the the popular La Jolla Cove is a small artificial cove on a point of land that is protected from the swells by a small sea wall. The small breakwater was erected to create a calm pool of ocean that children could safely play in; hence, the given name of "Children's Pool."

   Also known to many as Casa Pool, the tiny calm bay is an excellent jumping-off point for diving nearby reefs. Depths on the reefs average from 10 to 30 feet, most of them running parallel to shore and 20 feet high in some locations. Extreme undercutting on the reefs has created huge ledges that are a delight to explore, with sand and small boulders that also hold a variety of marine life.

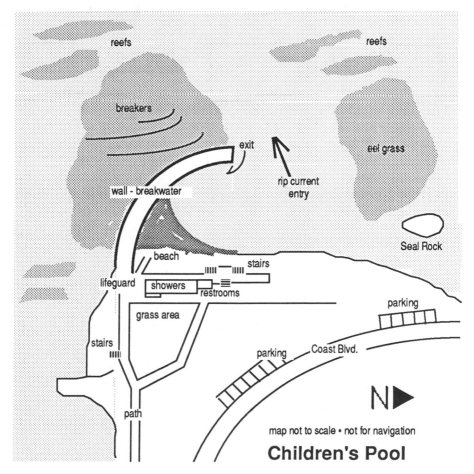

Children's Pool

map not to scale • not for navigation

In the shallow portions, eel grass grows prolifically. On the ledges and rocks, it is not unusual to find colorful anemones, sponges, starfish, nudibranchs and a number of types of mollusks. The fish surrounding the reef include garibaldi, senoritas, opaleye, and other reef-dwelling fish. Lucky divers sometimes spot groupers that are returning to the area. Playful seals are also common visitors to the area.

Hunting the reefs off Children's Pool is not very productive due to the heavy pressure from divers. An occasional lobster and abalone can be found on the outer reefs, with lobster also hiding in the eel grass in shallow water. Game fish present include sheephead, calico bass, and halibut; a rare white sea bass has been known to cruise the outer waters. Taking spears and spearguns through the pool when crowded is

discouraged.

As previously stated, Casa Pool is located less than a half mile south of La Jolla Cove along Coast Boulevard. Parking along Coast Boulevard is limited and allows for a maximum of three hours only. The beach here is plagued with crowds that almost equal those at La Jolla Cove. Try to arrive in the early mornings or weekdays or both.

There is a good dive-staging area directly behind the lifeguard headquarters. Below these headquarters are restrooms, showers, and a drinking fountain. Behind the lifeguard tower are telephones. The ledge at the lifeguard tower overlooks the small sandy cove. There are reefs outside the wall and directly out from Seal Rock that lies in front of the cove.

Behind the park, to the south, is Casa Cove; this spot is another good dive location on calm days but is open to southery swells in the summer.

Entry at Children's Pool is off the small sandy beach. There is a strong prevailing rip that runs out from the end of the wall which can be an express ticket to the reefs. Returning to the cove is best done by swimming very close to the tip of the wall where there is no rip and the surge will shove you back into the small cove.

Check with the lifeguard tower before entering. Up-to-date conditions are posted on the chalkboard outside. If unfamiliar with the area, the lifeguard will be happy to answer any questions.

Hospital Point

The entire area of La Jolla is surrounded by excellent diving. La Jolla Cove and Children's Pool are excellent dive locations but crowds and parking are a problem. By heading south along the west-facing beaches, some of the crowds can be avoided. One of the best best beach-diving spots of these shores lies off Hospital Point.

Noted to be especially good for visibility, only La Jolla Cove and Children's Pool to the north better it. In good conditions, visibility runs 15 to 30 feet and the clear water contains a good variety of life. Morays, bottom fish, octopus, an occasional lobster, and, if you're lucky, abalone, can be found on the bottom offshore from the point.

Hospital Point (sometimes called Whale View Point) is actually not a specific point but a large rocky area less than 1/2 mile south of Children's Pool Beach. There are a number of possible entry points along this rocky shore but the one most widely used by local divers and generally considered the easiest is across from 417 Coast Boulevard. There are short stairs to the beach here and a small sandy beach from which to enter. Two hours of free parking is available along Coast Blvd.

Entry is no problem with little or no surf but can be hazardous with anything bigger due to small shallow reefs that are exposed at low tide. Channels can

also creates a rip problem. Diving in this area is best at high tide.

The bottom is very shallow to about 30 to 40 yards out where a ledge drops into deeper water and better diving. The bottom then gently slopes to 40 feet deep 300 yards out. The bottom contains reefs with ledges interspersed with sand channels. Most of the reefs are parallel to shore and are anywhere from four to ten feet in height. There is even a small underwater arch that a diver can fit through.

Even with moderate surf, surge can be a problem. It's possible to escape some effects of the surge by remaining low in the channels between the reefs.

There are no facilities here but parking is usually no problem on all but the most crowded days. There are a few picnic benches and barbeque pits nearby.

North Mission Beach Jetty

It seems most divers are always looking for a good dive spot to pluck an abalone or grab a lobster. Unfortunately, many of us don't have the time to head out for the islands where both of these highly edible invertebrates are common. Alas, we are committed to searching for them along the coast. A spot San Diegans may wish to consider is the North Mission Beach Jetty.

Although not in abundant numbers, both lobster and black abalone can be found among these jumbled boulders.

But, before you become completely sold on this dive spot you need to know that it is a popular surfing spot as well. The surf zone is wide and large waves are not unusual. You can, however, bypass much of this problem by hoofing it out across the boulders along the jetty and making a water entry off the rocks. Although you definitely need experience with this type of entry, there are a number of good entry spots two-thirds to three-quarters of the way out along the jetty. With the right spot, surf conditions of three feet or less, and good timing between the wave sets, water entry should not be difficult.

The jumbled rock boulders create an excellent habitat to explore. Look into the deep holes and ledges for lobster. Black abalone are harder to find and most commonly found in narrow crevices in shallow water of 15 feet or less. Black abalone are considered the least desirable of the abalone family but they do make an excellent chowder base or a good, albeit chewy, abalone steak.

Game hunters will also find halibut in the sand during the spring and summer and kelp bass, small sheephead, and rockfish in the rocks. Digging in the sand may also yield a pismo clam or two.

The water depth along the jetty is fairly shallow reaching a maximum of only a little over 20 feet at the tip. Because of this, surge can be a problem. This can best be avoided by diving here during periods of low surf. Visibility is variable, depending on conditions. 5 to 15 feet is about average with 25 feet being tops.

Photographers had best leave their cameras at home. There is plenty to photograph and see, but the risk of hauling your camera across boulders, through a rock surf entry, and having it pushed around in the surge may be just too great for the possible reward.

Facilities at North Mission Beach Jetty are excellent. There is a large lifeguard tower that is almost always manned. Parking is abundant in all but the busiest summer months and there are full restroom and shower facilities. There are even a few fire pits along the beach and inside the jetty.

Although this can be a tough dive, do not be tempted to dive inside the breakwater; this is strictly prohibited and there are dangers presented by heavy boat traffic.